More Everyday Wisdom

BACKPACKER
The Magazine Of Wilderness Travel

More Everyday Wisdom

by Karen Berger

Photos by Karen Berger and Daniel R. Smith

THE MOUNTAINEERS BOOKS

Published by
The Mountaineers Books
1001 SW Klickitat Way, Suite 201
Seattle, WA 98134

First edition, 2002

Published simultaneously in Great Britain by Cordee, 3a DeMontfort Street, Leicester, England, LE1 7HD

Manufactured in the United States of America

Project Editor: David Emblidge
Editor: Jane Crosen
Cover and Book Design: Ani Rucki
Layout: Jennifer LaRock Shontz

All photos by Karen Berger and Daniel R. Smith

Cover photograph © Rob Bossi
Frontispiece: *The author uses a topographic map and a compass to identify her location on the Arizona Trail.*

Library of Congress Cataloging-in-Publication Data
Berger, Karen, 1959–
    More everyday wisdom : trail-tested advice from the experts / by Karen
Berger.—1st ed.
        p.   cm.
Includes bibliographical references and index.
ISBN 0-89886-899-8 (pbk.)
1. Hiking. 2. Backpacking. I. Title: Everyday wisdom. II. Title.
GV199.5 .B475 2002
796.51—dc21
                                                              2002013027

Table of Contents

Introduction

This book is, very simply, the result of talking to many people over many years about a subject that I love: traveling on foot through wilderness.

I didn't set out to become a hiking writer, or a writing hiker. It was much more simple than that.

I love to hike, and I love to write. You can't ask more out of life than to find a job that pays you to do what you love. I got lucky: Writing and hiking dovetailed perfectly when I received a contract for my first book, a travelogue about walking the Continental Divide from Mexico to Canada.

More hikes, and more books, followed. As I continued to hike, and to write about it, I met people on trails, in classes, in lecture halls, on the Internet. I exchanged ideas about gear, about minimum-impact camping, about coping with hiking partners, about mileage and lightweight techniques, about whether to mark trails, and about controversies like cell phones and dogs and guns and wildlands preservation. I learned a lot. And I answered questions.

Dozens and dozens of questions.

As it turns out, the basic how-to books (my own books included) can't answer all the questions people actually ask in the field. Sometimes, those of us who write these books forget the questions we had when we first started. Sometimes, there just isn't enough space. Sometimes other people come up with a question we wouldn't think of in a million years.

I've been keeping track of the questions over the last few years. Initially, answering questions helped me to meet the needs of readers when I wrote books and articles for magazines and the Internet. But as time passed and the questions piled up, I realized that what readers had given me was the outline for a whole other book, a book that addressed the issues hikers *really* want to know about.

Of course, no single book can answer every question that any hiker could ever ask. Some questions are so highly specific to a particular trail or an individual's unique situation that they would be of limited interest to others. And some common questions are answered in many of the fine how-to backpacking books already on the market.

Why hike? For the views, of course. (View of the Grand Canyon, Arizona.)

For this book, I've chosen to answer questions that fall into several categories: Questions that make people sit up and say, "I've always wondered that, too." Questions whose answers make life in the backcountry easier and more pleasant. And questions that many people ask.

Some of these questions you may have asked yourself. Some you already know the answers to. And some you may never have even considered.

Have you ever wondered whether and where it's possible to hike without having to carry all your gear? Have you ever questioned why horseback riders get the right-of-way? Do you know why people start climbing mountains in the middle of the night? Do you know how to predict the weather by the shape of the clouds and the smell of the forest? Do you know what to do if a grouse attacks you (yes, a grouse)? Or a grizzly bear? Or what to do if you encounter a snake, a porcupine, a skunk, a mountain lion?

Do you know . . .

▲ The differences between East Coast hiking and West Coast hiking?
▲ How new airline security regulations affect the gear you might take on a plane?
▲ What climbing ratings mean?
▲ How much money long-distance hikers spend?
▲ How to make backcountry coffee?
▲ How much food you need to carry per day?
▲ How to calculate mileage from a map?
▲ How much a lightweight tent should weigh?
▲ How to rescue a tired old sleeping bag?
▲ How many miles a pair of boots is good for?

Every one of these questions has been asked by a reader, someone attending a workshop, or a hiker on a trail. I'm not telling you what I think you should know; I'm answering the questions people *really* ask.

So where should we start?

Perhaps my favorite question ever came courtesy of an Internet site I wrote for. One reader simply wanted to know: Why hike? My answer was a little tongue-in-cheek—but serious, too. Hiking is, after all, about joy.

Here's what she asked:

It seems there's so much planning and equipment involved in getting started. I'm wondering if it's worth the investment. What are some of the advantages of hiking or backpacking?

Here's how I answered:

Let's see, I'm guessing you already know that backpacking is great exercise. (In fact, by hauling yourself and pack up and down mountains, you can burn off 4000 or more calories a day.) I'm assuming you know that it feels good to climb a mountain and finally get to the top; also, that hiking can take you to places you've only seen in the pages of *National Geographic* magazine.

I figure that you already know that a dose of nature is just what the doctor ordered after a week in the workplace: the chance to watch a flower bloom, or chase a snowflake, or gape at the northern lights. And I know you know that hiking is a great activity for people of any age—so you can spend quality family time in a quality place.

So let's get down to the serious stuff, the nitty-gritty advantages that'll have you breaking out that credit card at your local outdoor store and earning enough frequent-buyer dividends to purchase a four-season mountaineering tent with change left over for a super-deluxe inflatable mattress.

Here they are: Top 15 Reasons to Hike

- ▲ You can eat all you want and still lose weight.
- ▲ Your boss doesn't come with you.
- ▲ You can honestly say, "No I didn't get your message—there was no cell phone reception in Dead Horse Gulch."
- ▲ It gives you a good excuse to sleep for 10 hours straight. You're exhausted, and besides, it's dark out.
- ▲ Nobody will try to sell you insurance.
- ▲ Everything tastes better after you've walked 10 miles.
- ▲ You can actually find something to *do* with the scissors, nail file, sawing blade, and power screwdriver on your Swiss army knife. (What d'ya mean, yours doesn't have a power screwdriver?)
- ▲ Nobody will think you're dressed stupid, even if you wear shorts over your long underwear.
- ▲ You can spend all kinds of money on bright-colored technical gear while telling yourself you really need this stuff. I mean, we're talking survival here.
- ▲ Backcountry cappuccino machine? Titanium tent stakes? This year, when your relatives ask what you want for Christmas, you'll have a list to give them.
- ▲ You will remember what air smells like when it's not saturated with exhaust fumes.
- ▲ You will remember what silence sounds like.
- ▲ And birds.
- ▲ You will feel a sense of real satisfaction when you realize that you can live without hot showers, running water, a soft bed, and with so little stuff that you can carry it around on your back.
- ▲ When you return back home, you will feel a sense of real satisfaction that you have hot showers, running water, a soft bed, and so much stuff that you couldn't possibly carry it all around on your back.

For more questions, and more answers, read on. And if, by the end of the book, I haven't answered yours, please visit me at *www.hikerwriter.com*.

Chapter 1

How to Plan
GETTING TO THE TRAILHEAD

lanning a hike is like planning anything else in life: It requires deciding what you want to do, learning as much as you can about it, and making sure you have the skills and equipment you need. Beyond that, how you plan, and how much you plan, has more to do with how flexible and spontaneous you are, and how you feel about surprises.

With hiking, it helps to know a little about the lay of the land, where to find information about hiking trails and maps, and how to develop your skills. It also helps to know about issues like transportation around trailheads, carting hiking equipment on planes, permits, and expenses.

The sidebars in this chapter offer contact information for the major organizations, parks, and forests discussed in the text. For trail clubs not listed in sidebars, contact the American Hiking Society:
www.americanhiking.org/alliance/members.html.

Getting Started.

Q. I want to go on a weekend backpacking trip, but I have no idea how plan it. How do I find a trail? How do I know where to camp?

A. No matter where you live, there's a hiking trail nearby. You'll find opportunities to hike in national forests and national parks, in state and county parks and preserves, in Bureau of Land Management lands, and in wildlife refuges; you can get specific information about trails, regulations, and maps from agencies that manage these public lands. Maps and guidebooks covering nearby destinations are often available at outdoor retailers, where the sales staff is made up of outdoorspeople who hike and camp themselves. Stores may also offer public bulletin boards containing information about local clubs, activities, and parks. The Internet is another source of information. A little surfing will bring you to trail descriptions, agency websites, hiking clubs, and online bookstores.

For a weekend, you probably want to maximize your trail time and minimize your drive time, so figure no more than 2 or 3 hours by car. The Appalachian and Pacific Crest Trails are two places to start because they are supported by informative trail organizations and they are well marked. Since the majority of the U.S. population lives on (or near) the West and East Coasts, most of us live within a 3-hour drive of some part of one of these two trails, making it easy to hike a section over a weekend.

Other sources of information are trail clubs, which often sponsor group hikes, maintain trails, and can provide enough information to keep you hiking for years to come. You can find a hiking club in your area by going to the American Hiking Society website.

Another good resource is the DeLorme atlas series, now available for most states. They provide an overview of regional hiking possibilities, camping accommodations, and trailhead access.

Once you've picked a place to hike, planning is all about making the trip more comfortable. You'll need to know how long the hike will take, how much food you'll need, how difficult the trail is, whether there are any environmental complications like snowfields or long stretches with no water, and how many miles a day you'll cover. Be sure to consider how much time you have and what kind of shape you're in. If you've been sitting at the computer all winter, plan to hike no more than 6 to 10 miles a day, depending on the difficulty of the trail. If you've just run the New York marathon, you can let yourself be more ambitious, but not too ambitious—15 miles is plenty even for the super-fit. (You'll be carrying a pack, and hiking uses different muscles.)

Beyond that, how much planning you do is up to you. Planning is more important in more rigorous terrain—for example, in drylands, where water is limited, or on trails that traverse steep slopes where camping may be impossible for many miles at a time. Many people like the security of knowing in advance where their target campsites will be. Some, however, prefer to "go with the flow."

Finally, discuss your plans with your hiking partner (you should have one, at least until you are confident in your outdoor skills). For more on hiking partners, see Chapter 7.

Developing Skills.

Q. I want to develop my outdoors skills in order to be able to handle more challenging terrain. Where do I begin?

A. You can sharpen your backcountry skills by hooking up with like-minded people, taking classes, and (of course) reading books.

Start by hiking over to an outfitting store, which might post notices of local activities and hikes on its bulletin board. Sometimes, outfitters offer classes and workshops themselves.

Many trail clubs also offer classes and trips. National organizations such as the Sierra Club are famous for worldwide expeditions, but local chapters offer local rambles, too. Organizations such as the Appalachian Mountain Club (the Northeast), the Mazamas (Oregon), The Mountaineers (Washington), Keystone Trails (Pennsylvania), the Potomac Appalachian Trail Club (Washington, D.C. area), and the Colorado Mountain Club also offer programs where you'll pick up skills—and maybe even a hiking partner or two. Some trail clubs and hiking groups have annual events featuring dozens of slide shows, lectures, and classes covering everything from hiking in Antarctica to ultralight camping in California's Mojave Desert.

Experience is the best teacher. Get used to going out in different kinds of weather, even if it's only for an hour or two—exposure to rain and snow will help you decide what kind of gear to pack when you decide it's time to go overnight.

Planning Checklist

▲ Check with the agency that manages the trails you'll be hiking to see if they require permits, which you might need to apply for in advance. Other questions to ask: Is there any particular gear they recommend? Are there any seasonal considerations you need to be aware of? Are there unusual challenges such as a high snow accumulation or relocations due to forest fire damage?

▲ Make a gear list (see Chapter 4). Keep notes on which items you took on which hikes, which gear you used, and which gear you could have left at home. In the future, you can refer to the list and pack more efficiently.

▲ Check with your partner. You don't each need an army knife, stove, tent, first-aid kit, and water filter. Sharing is a great opportunity to shed some weight.

▲ Get all your gear together and check its condition to be sure nothing is falling apart and no parts are missing. (I've shown up on trails minus the hipbelt buckle for a pack and the pump for a stove.)

▲ If you haven't been hiking in a while, it's a good idea to take a few training walks wearing your boots. It'll help you break them in—and avoid blisters on the trail.

▲ Plan menus, shop for food, package and send on any food drops, and pack the food items you'll carry with you. Take one last look in the refrigerator to be sure you haven't forgotten anything!

Hiking trails are found on many different kinds of land. The alphabet soup of land management agencies can be daunting to the uninitiated.

▲ National forests are within the U.S. Department of Agriculture. Most are managed for multiple use, including logging, mining, grazing, and many kinds of recreation.

▲ National parks include national parks, monuments, seashores, lakeshores, grasslands, historic sites, and others. Information on national parks can be found at *www.nps.gov*.

▲ National wildlife refuges are managed by the U.S. Department of Fish and Wildlife, Department of the Interior. While primarily managed as habitats for wildlife, they also offer many miles of hiking trails and other recreational opportunities.

▲ The Department of the Interior's Bureau of Land Management manages millions of acres of public multiple-use land. Grazing, logging, and mining are common uses, but many BLM lands have hiking trails, too.

▲ Wilderness areas are usually found on USDA Forest Service lands, although parts of national parks and BLM lands may also be managed as protected wildernesses.

▲ State parks may offer everything from swimming areas to tennis courts, and rental cabins to backpacking.

▲ County and city parks also offer close-to-home hiking opportunities. Check with your local department of recreation.

▲ Thanks to the efforts of national and regional land trusts and conservation groups, a growing number of nature preserves also offer public access and hiking trails.

Finally, check out a couple of basic backpacking books—there are plenty of good ones on the market, as well as outdoor magazines that provide up-to-date information on gear and skills.

Likes Hiking, Hates Hauling.

Q. I love to walk, but I'm not a camper. Where can I get information for a more luxury-style hike where I could stay at inns at night?

A. One choice is to look for loop hikes that start and end near rural lodges and resorts. You'll find backcountry lodges located right next to national forests and state and national parks, ranging from cozy B&Bs to luxury lodges to rustic cabins. You can find these lodgings by calling chambers of commerce in towns near the park or forest where you'd like to hike.

Proprietors of rural lodgings can often recommend hikes in the area. Or you can check a forest map to see if there are nearby loop hikes that bring you back to the same place at night.

If you like hiking with other people, you might look for a van-supported hike offered by a hiking or environmental organization. The Colorado Trail Foundation, for example, runs supported trips on the Colorado Trail. We're not exactly talking four-star luxury, but you don't have to haul all your gear and food. Organizations such as Elderhostel also run supported hiking trips. So do commercial companies. To find them, look in the back of major outdoor magazines.

If you're interested in solo travel, check out the Appalachian Trail, where local hotel and inn owners are used to hosting hikers. The annual *Appalachian Trail Thru-Hikers' Companion*, available from the Appalachian Trail Conference (304-535-6331), lists hotels, inns, and B&Bs that are near the trail. For example, in Maine it is possible to hike from one road crossing to the next and arrange to be picked up each evening by the owners of various hiker-friendly B&Bs. The PCT sells a similar guide to trail towns; however, the larger distances between road crossings on the PCT make it difficult to hike from one lodging to the next in a day.

Another option is to use backcountry huts, where they exist. You'll need to carry clothing and personal items. In some hut systems, depending on what services are offered, you also need to carry sleeping bags, food, and a stove.

Backcountry huts range from simple cabins to beautiful mountain chalets. Some examples:

▲ Colorado's 10th Mountain Division Huts include twenty-four huts between Aspen, Leadville, and Vail, all above 9700 feet. Many of these huts are lovely chalet-style lodgings where you cook your own meals. You can get more info—as well as information about other Colorado hut systems—at *www.huts.org*.

▲ In the East, the Appalachian Mountain Club runs a hut system in the White Mountains. Lodging is dormitory style. In some huts, food is served; in others, it's self-service. Reservations are required (603-466-2727). More basic backcountry accommodations are offered by the Randolph Mountain Club (also in the White Mountains). For more information, visit *www.randolphmountainclub.org*.

▲ The Potomac Appalachian Trail Club Trail in the Washington, D.C. area also maintains a system of huts for members. Find them on the web at *www.patc.net*.

▲ For a list of other huts and hut systems in the United States and Canada, check out *www.powderbuzz.com*.

Finally, why not travel abroad? European trails have well-developed systems of B&Bs and backcountry huts. Hut systems are so popular in the Alps that "wild camping" (as the Europeans call it) is almost unheard of! You can walk across entire countries without ever pitching a tent. On some of these trails, like England's Coast-to-Coast Walk, you can stay in B&Bs every night and you can even arrange for a local commercial service to transport your luggage from one town to the next. On other trails, like the GR-10, which zigzags about 600 miles across the French Pyrenees, you can choose between in-town lodgings and backcountry refuges. You could also try tramping (as it's called) in New Zealand, a country with literally hundreds of backcountry huts.

Some European hiking clubs run comfortable hotels, such as the GR 5 atop the Grand Ballon in Alsace, France.

Finding Your Way to the Right Maps.

Q. I'm new at hiking, backpacking, and camping. What kind of maps do I need and where do I find them?

A. Several different kinds of maps are commonly used in hiking and backpacking.

Often, the maps you'll find in a guidebook will suffice. On well-marked trails, you don't usually need maps to find your way because you can just follow the footway. Here, you are more likely to use maps to double-check where you are, how far you have to go, or what the terrain ahead might look like. For example, a map would warn you about a 1000-foot climb at the end of the day. Maps can also help you plan stops for water and campsites.

If guidebooks aren't available, or if their maps are of poor quality, you might need some of the following kinds of maps.

In New England's Appalachian Mountain Club huts, hikers sleep in dormitories and are served three-course meals (Lakes of the Clouds Hut, New Hampshire).

Forest Service maps. These are small-scale maps (usually about 1:100,000; in other words, 1 centimeter on the map equals 1 kilometer on the ground). These maps lack topographic information such as contour lines (which provide information about steepness, climbs, and changing elevations). They are useful if you're going long distances, but because they cover a lot of ground in a small amount of space, they are insufficient for cross-country travel. Forest Service maps are available from national forest supervisors' offices and ranger stations.

BLM maps. Similar to Forest Service maps, these are usually small-scale maps containing some topographic information about areas managed by the Bureau of Land Management.

Park Service and Wilderness maps. Designed with hikers and other recreationists in mind, these topographic maps are usually scaled at about 1:50,000, a convenient scale for hiking because it allows the map to cover several miles while providing enough detail for a traveler on foot. Some commercial companies produce similar maps (some are waterproof) of popular recreation areas.

USGS topographic maps. Published by the United States Geological Survey, usually at a scale of 1:25,000, these contain the most detail commonly available—probably more detail than you need on a well-marked trail, but they are excellent for off-trail travel. They note features of interest to hikers such as trails, springs, and back roads. Note that on older maps, these features are often out of date. Topo maps are available from the USGS (1-800-HELP-MAP), and often from retailers in the area.

Permits and Regulations.

Q. Do I have to make plans with some sort of office to let them know where I'm going to be hiking, or can I just park the car and disappear into the woods?

A. Although in many cases you can just disappear into the woods, there are exceptions.

Most national parks require hikers to have backcountry permits. Some permits limit you to specific trails or particular campsites. Sometimes these rules are designed to manage the flow of visitors; sometimes they are safety related. In Yellowstone and Glacier National Parks, for example, hikers are required to stay in designated campsites clustered together because grizzly bears will avoid groups.

Permits are also required in some wilderness areas, usually on a walk-in basis. You don't have to make arrangements in advance; you simply fill in a form at a trailhead registration box. This helps the rangers evaluate trail traffic and better manage the area.

Some agencies charge trailhead parking fees; parking stickers may only be available at ranger stations. You can find out whether parking or backcountry permits are required by calling the land management agency (usually, a national forest ranger station or a national park backcountry office). Regardless of whether permits are required, it's a good idea to check in with rangers before you start your hike. Rangers can apprise you of local conditions and can recommend trails that are suitable for your level of experience and the equipment you are carrying. Registering at a ranger station also helps rescuers to find you in case of an emergency.

Getting Back to the Car.

Q. When my wife and I hike, we drive to the trailhead. How do you get back to your starting point after a week on the trail? Seeing the same country from a different perspective is nice, but we don't want to backtrack.

A. When you hike in a straight line from Point A to Point B, getting back to your car can be tricky because public transportation in America's remote countryside is spotty at best. One of the best ways to avoid this problem is to hike in a loop: a trail that goes in a big circle. Some loop trails include the Wonderland Trail around Washington's Mount Rainier, the Susquenhannock Trail in Pennsylvania, and (for the ambitious) the Buckeye Trail, which circles the state of Ohio. You can also form your own loop by linking a series of trails.

In some popular hiking areas, there may be services like public buses and hiker shuttles. New England's Appalachian Mountain Club, for example,

Hiking in a group is safer when dealing with obstacles like stream crossings (Continental Divide Trail, Montana).

runs vans between White Mountain trailheads on a regular schedule. Similar services are offered in some national parks. Local public transportation may also be an option; check with the chamber of commerce.

Some trail clubs maintain lists of people who will shuttle cars for hikers, often for a small fee. You park your car at one end of the trail; the shuttler drives you to the other end. Then you simply walk back to your car. You might also be able to park at a local business (like a store or a motel) near the trail. Don't be afraid to ask; many trailside businesses are used to the myriad needs of hikers, and some will even drive you to the trailhead.

Hitchhiking to Trailheads.

Q. I'm planning a long hike, but the towns where I want to resupply are sometimes several miles from the trail. Do I have to hitchhike?

A. Hitchhiking was once a pretty reliable way to get yourself a few miles down a country road, but it has become more and more dangerous in recent years. Sometimes you can avoid hitchhiking by hiking an alternate trail into a town. Sometimes you may not have a choice. To maximize your chance of a safe ride:

- ▲ Beg. Day hikers park their cars at trailheads. Look for a fellow hiker who's coming out of the woods, and ask for a ride.

- Use your cell phone to call a taxi service. Or, if you're staying at a local B&B, the owner might be willing to run you to and from the trailhead.
- Hook up with another hiker. Hitching with a partner is safer than hitching alone (see also "Personal Safety," Chapter 7).
- Ride in the back of pickup trucks, where you are less vulnerable.
- If you have to be separated from your gear, keep your money and valuables on you.

Can Fuel Fly?

Q. My husband and I are going to southern Utah to backpack in the national parks. Our stove uses propane-butane gas canisters, and we have heard that we cannot bring them on the plane with us. How do people transport their cooking fuel?

A. You cannot bring stove fuel on a plane.

You can send gas canisters via UPS if you specify ground shipment *only.* (Allow plenty of time.) You would need to find an address that would receive and hold your package for you. If you'll be spending your first night in a hotel, you could have the canister shipped there.

It may not be necessary to go to all that trouble. Shops in national parks usually sell common stove fuels, as do stores in towns near major recreation areas. You could call the park before you go, ask for the phone number of the concessionaire who runs the store, and double-check that they sell the type of fuel you need.

More Airline Regulations.

Q. How do the new security procedures in airports affect outdoor travelers? Can I still pack a stove in my luggage? How about equipment like Swiss army knives?

A. The best (and most hassle-free) way to fly these days is to check everything except for your money, your personal essentials, and your boots.

Hiking poles, pocket knives, ice axes, crampons, ice screws, and tent stakes are all going to cause problems at the security gate—but they can go in checked luggage. (Hiking sticks should be collapsible, or they won't fit.) Airlines have inconsistent policies regarding stoves, so it's best to check in advance with the airline. If in doubt, send the stove ahead to general delivery at a post office near the airport and pick it up when you get there.

As far as your boots are concerned, there's no regulation (yet!) about stinky boots on planes. I recommend carrying them on because they are the most difficult piece of gear to replace if your gear gets lost in transit.

Why hike? To feel like this (Gila Wilderness, New Mexico).

Your Backpack versus the Luggage Handlers.

Q. I'm planning to go on an overseas trip. I've seen plenty of exploded backpacks come off the luggage carousels. How do I prevent this from happening?

A. Backpacks are vulnerable. They don't lock, and both the frames and the straps can be damaged during careless handling. Essentially, there are two ways to protect your pack when checking it onto a plane:

▲ Pack it in something else, like a duffel bag. If you're staying at the same hotel at the beginning and end of your trip, you can usually make arrangements for the hotel to hold your duffel bag for you, along with any city clothes you might not want to take backpacking. If you plan to end your hike in a different city, you can simply ship the duffel bag to the hotel where you'll be staying.

▲ Or, if you don't want to deal with shipping a duffel, you can still make your pack travel-ready. Remove all removable straps and buckles (often, this includes the shoulder harness and the hipbelt) and pack them inside. Tighten straps that remain, then tuck in or tie off any loose ends. You could additionally wrap the pack in garbage bags that are taped in place with lots and lots of duct tape. Tie rope securely around the whole package to hold it together and give the baggage handlers something to hold.

Help! I Can't Find the Trail!

Q. Several times I have tried to find a "well-marked trailhead" with no success. Is there something I'm missing?

A. I have to admit I have the same problem. Trailheads—even ones you know—can be hard to spot from a moving vehicle.

Here's what I do when I'm hunting for a trailhead.

First, I get directions from the ranger station or land management agency. Sometimes, maps don't exactly match what you'll see on the ground. Small back roads may be omitted from the maps or may have been renumbered. I ask how far the trailhead is from the nearest junction and if there's any obvious way to know if I've gone too far. I also ask how the trail is blazed—is it marked with paint blazes of a certain color, or by ax-blazes cut into the bark of trees?

Second, I drive slowly, looking for areas where people have obviously parked. Parked cars are a dead giveaway that there's a trail in the area.

Third, I don't expect to find a big fancy kiosk and picnic shelter. Some trailheads have information boards and outhouses and garbage bins, but many are little more than a few parking places and a trail sign that you might not even see until you get out of the car and scout around.

One of the reasons the Appalachian Trail is so popular is that it's well-marked, making it easy for beginners to find the way (Appalachian Trail, New Hampshire).

What Do Climbing Ratings Mean?

Q. We are three fortyish amigos planning our second-ever hiking trip. People have described the trail we want to hike as a "Class 3 climb." What does this mean? Is this something a careful person with no mountaineering training should attempt?

A. Your friends are using the Yosemite Decimal System, which is the most commonly used system for rating climbs. Here's how it works:

Class 1 isn't really a climb at all—it's merely hiking (perhaps occasionally tripping over a few rocks).

Class 2 is what people might refer to as off-trail hiking. Examples would include scrambling on scree and talus (the rocky debris found on mountains), where you might occasionally have to use your hands for balance or leverage.

Class 3 means scrambling for real. You need to use your arms as well as your legs, and there might be some exposure where a fall could result in broken bones. Ropes are not required. Sometimes, cables will be placed in rocks to aid in giving you handholds.

Class 4 means that the exposure is serious enough to require a belay (a rope worn around your waist and held by another hiker).

Class 5 means that a leader has to place protection (devices that are put into the rock to hold a rope). These are the climbs you read about in climbing magazines. Class 5 is divided into further subcategories (5.0, 5.1, and so on) depending on difficulty (basically from the merely impossible to the totally inconceivable!).

Class 6 is aid climbing, using both ropes and fixtures like cables and bolts permanently embedded in the rock.

It's not uncommon to find Class 3 climbs on a hiking trail. An example would be the infamous Mahoosuc Notch on the Appalachian Trail in Maine—which is mostly an "easy" Class 3. Hikers have to scramble over, around, through, and under an obstacle course of rocks, sometimes taking their packs off and passing them to one another. I've never seen anyone using a rope there, and plenty of beginners make it through just fine, but people do fall and injuries do occur.

Deciding whether you're up for Class 3 is really a judgment call, based on your own abilities, balance, and fear of heights. You don't need mountaineering training or technical aids—but you do need to be fit, confident, and careful. Once you've done a bunch of scrambling, you start learning how to move your body so it stays in balance. At the beginning, some people have a little difficulty. It's an individual thing, like learning math or playing the piano. If you're not confident of your balance, you might want to check out a climbing wall close to home just to get the feeling of using your arms and legs together.

For more information on climbing, check out *Mountaineering: Freedom of the Hills* (The Mountaineers Books, 1997).

How Hard Is the Hike?

Q. How can I evaluate the difficulty of a hike before I get in over my head?

A. First realize that "hard" means different things to different people. To some people, river fords are hard and snowfields are easy. To others, long mileage is a snap, but ascending mountains is a strain. So "know thyself" is some good first advice.

Realize that there isn't a single trail rating system. Some clubs rate trails as "easy," "moderate," and "difficult," but these ratings can vary considerably from club to club; you'll have to find out for yourself what they actually mean to you.

Guidebooks and maps often contain good information. Forest Service and Park Service maps usually discuss environmental factors and physical challenges. A quick call to a ranger station or trail club can also alert you to problems and difficulties. Here's what to look for:

▲ Contour lines close together on a map means a lot of up and down; the closer the lines, the steeper the climb.

▲ Footway information—clambering over rocks, scrambling on scree, swampy mud—won't be marked on a map, so you'll have to read a guidebook or ask a ranger.

▲ Above tree line, exposure to high winds and weather presents a danger in bad weather. Dealing with in-your-face weather that stays in your face all day can be tiring.

▲ Obstacles like snowfields and river fords can slow down your progress to a mile an hour or even less. These obstacles are often seasonal, and should be discussed in a guidebook.

▲ Navigation can also pose problems. If the trail isn't well marked, you'll need good skills, and you'll need to factor in extra time.

Dollars per Mile.

Q. I've always wanted to do a long hike. How much does long-distance hiking cost?

A. The initial outlay can seem expensive, especially if you need to buy all your gear from scratch. Expect to spend at least $1000–$1200 on the basics: tent, sleeping bag, pack, boots, stove, and raingear. That budget will get you

A class 3 scramble requires confidence (Mahoosuc Notch, Maine).

solid middle-of-the-road equipment, but nothing fancy. High rollers can easily spend $500 more. Figure another $300–$400 for clothing, pots, eating utensils, first aid and personal gear, maps, and guidebooks. Transportation to and from the trailhead is a variable expense, depending on where you live, where the trailheads are, and how you plan to travel. Finally, there's food, postage for resupply boxes, plus money for layover days in town.

Food costs vary depending on whether you dehydrate your own food, use packaged foods commonly available in supermarkets, shop at a bulk-rate coop, or buy more expensive freeze-dried foods (discounts are sometimes available if you buy large quantities). Snacks like cereal bars and nutrition bars can raise the total considerably. My food drops usually contain a wide variety. A typical 5-day food drop for one person might cost around $40 (this doesn't include last-minute perishable items, like cheese and meat, which I buy when I pick up the package). Postage costs for shipping these supplies can add up quickly, too, especially over long distances.

Ready for some good news? Once you've bought your gear, your ticket (or other transportation costs), and most of the food you'll send to yourself, there isn't much left to spend money on. Hikers figure $1 to $2 a mile for on-trail expenses. (Another way to figure it is $100 per overnight town stop.)

There are ways to minimize the expenses. Some hikers make their own gear. Some cook and dehydrate most of their meals in advance. Some minimize their town expenses by staying in campgrounds and hostels rather than hotels. Couples or hiking partners can lower the tally by sharing expenses like the occasional motel room or postage for sending unneeded equipment home.

For thorough (if exhaustive) planning and cost-estimate worksheets, check out *The Thru-Hiker's Planning Guide* by Dan Bruce (Center for Appalachian Trail Studies, 1997). The guide is intended for AT hikers, but the worksheets can be used by hikers on any long-distance trail.

Chapter 2

Where to Hike
DESTINATIONS FOR
LONG AND SHORT DREAM HIKES

rom Montana to Florida, from Maine to Arizona, America is blessed with trails. You can walk the length or the breadth of the country on trails that pass through deserts, mountains, forests, and beaches. Some trails take you past historic sites; others venture into deep wilderness. Trails follow old Indian routes, animal migration paths, settlers' routes, and the beds of abandoned railways.

Even an entire book devoted to the topic of where to hike could only scratch the surface of our vast trail system. If you're like most hikers, you'll take most of your day hikes in parks and public lands near your home. You'll drive up to a few hours for a weekend getaway. And you'll carefully plan occasional backpacking vacations that may take you across the country, or abroad.

This chapter answers questions about the nature of trails in various parts of the country, and offers information on some perennial favorites, from Vermont's Long Trail to Washington's Wonderland Trail, from the Arizona Trail to the Florida Trail, from the Appalachians to the Pacific Crest.

East versus West.

Q. I'm planning a two-week trip and can't decide on a location. I can't even decide whether to hike in the East or the West. What are some of the differences between Eastern hiking and Western hiking?

Tennessee's Balds prove that not all of the East Coast is covered in deciduous forest. (Hump Mountain, Tennessee).

A. Dividing the country into East and West invites some broad generalizations—many of which are only superficially true. After all, when you talk about the West, you're lumping the Sonoran Desert of Arizona with the High Sierra of California and the old-growth forests of the Pacific Northwest. The East is more homogeneous, with a large band of deciduous forest, but you also have the subtropical Florida Trail as well as the arctic-alpine environment of high peaks in New England and northern New York.

The Appalachian Trail is one of the most famous footpaths around, and many people assume that AT hiking is typical of all Eastern hiking. As a result, they think of Eastern trails as well blazed, with countless shelters, accessible only to foot-traffic (not bikes or horses). In fact, there are a lot of Eastern trails that don't fit that description at all.

That said, there are some generalizations you can make—as long as you remember that for every rule, there is an exception.

- Generalization: "There are shelters in the East, not in the West." Exception: Most Eastern shelters are found on a few major trails. And shelters *are* found, randomly, in the West— though admittedly, not many of them.
- Generalization: "When Eastern trails go up mountains, they switchback less than Western trails." Exception: Southeastern trails boast wonderful switchbacks, built by the Depression-era Civilian Conservation Corps (CCC). And there are some incredibly steep straight-up, straight-down trails in the West (one example: the Indian Springs Trail between the PCT and the Eagle Creek Trail in Oregon).
- Generalization: "Western wildernesses are more remote." Exception: While the West does boast our biggest and most remote wildernesses, many of its most popular hiking areas are accessible to major metropolitan centers. Examples include California's Desolation Wilderness and

Washington's Alpine Lakes Wilderness trailhead, where throngs fight for parking spaces on a sunny summer weekend.

I have pictures in my head of what Western hiking means, and I see big open spaces and high mountains and trails with huge changes in elevation. When I think of the East, I envision quiet green forests and trickling streams, "long green tunnels" that shine with bowers of rhododendron in the spring and blaze with foliage in the fall. But then it occurs to me: What about the Cascadian forests of the Northwest? Floridian cypress swamp? The bald open domes of Tennessee's Appalachians? Utah's slot canyons? And I become confused all over again.

A Big Trip.

Q. I'm planning a trip from the U.K. It's my first time in the United States. I'd like to visit some of America's great outdoor sites. Could you recommend a trail that would allow five to six weeks of walking with backcountry camping?

A. The United States is blessed with some of the most extraordinary scenery to be found anywhere in the world. Let me tell you about some of the places that show up most reliably in magazines and in surveys of hikers about their favorite places.

Going off the beaten track in the Grand Canyon yields better views and fewer people.

Wyoming's Wind River Range (in the Bridger–Teton National Forest) is near Grand Teton National Park, which gives you two spectacular places within a short distance of each other—not to mention Yellowstone National Park just to the north. The Wind River Range offers hundreds of miles of trails—you can follow the Continental Divide Trail for more than 100 miles from one end of the range to the other, and most of those miles are above 10,000 feet! You can also hike through Yellowstone National Park (although you'll probably want to rent a car while you're there in order to see all the "front country" natural wonders).

Two other incredible Rocky Mountain long hikes are the Continental Divide Trail in Colorado and the Colorado Trail. The Colorado CDT is longer (about 750 miles); the CT is "only" about 500. The CDT is higher (averaging more than 11,000 feet) and wilder, but on both trails, the views of range after range of snowcapped peaks are unsurpassed. Both require good backcountry skills, including map and compass.

John Muir called California's High Sierra the "Range of Light." It includes Sequoia, Kings Canyon, and Yosemite National Parks, and is one of our most spectacular places, with glaciated granite pinnacles reaching for the sky, 12,000 and 13,000-foot passes, and thousands of lakes and tarns. Following the Pacific Crest Trail, it's more than 350 awesome miles from Kennedy

A tour of the Southwest should include a day hike or backpacking trip in Bryce Canyon National Park.

Mount Rainier is the highest of the Northwest's Cascade volcanoes.

Meadows Campground (at the southern end of the South Sierra Wilderness) to Sonora Pass (near the north end of Yosemite National Park). North of Sonora Pass is beautiful as well—no reason not to keep going if you have the time! Or you can explore some of the High Sierra's other trails. The High Sierra also contains plenty of remote cross-country routes, where you can make your own trail if you have the skills.

Washington State also boasts a wide variety of trails, including 500 miles of the Pacific Crest Trail. On the PCT, you'll see the great volcanoes of the Pacific Northwest (Rainier, Adams, Mount St. Helens, and Glacier Peak), the craggy and snaggle-toothed North Cascades, and a smattering of awesome old-growth forests, including giant Douglas firs and Western red cedars. August is the best month for this hike. In Washington, you'll also find hundreds of miles of trails in the North Cascades National Park and in Olympic National Park, as well as the east–west-running Pacific Northwest Trail.

If you like deserts, a hiking tour of Arizona and Utah is also a treat. The 800-mile Arizona Trail includes a traverse of the Grand Canyon. Bryce Canyon, Arches, Zion, and Canyonlands National Parks are all nearby in Utah. Warning: Stay out of Arizona during the summer, when it's too hot to hike.

If you want to meet a lot of Americans, hiking any part of the Appalachian Trail will give you the opportunity to make lifelong friends and have a *lot* of fun. Quite honestly, the AT lacks the heart-stopping drama of the West, but it is one of the most popular trails in the world. The most spectacular sections are found in New England—although Tennessee, North Carolina, and Georgia hold their own in the scenery department, too.

U.S. Coast-to-Coast.

Q. Last summer I did the Coast-to-Coast Walk in England, and I became hooked on the idea of long-distance walks. Is there a way of walking coast-to-coast in the United States?

A. At the end of England's Coast-to-Coast Walk, there's a pub where hikers celebrate their achievement. In the hiker guest book I noted an entry (some might call it a challenge) from a fellow American walker: "We've done yours; now come do ours!" Forewarned is forearmed: "Ours" is about twenty times as long as "theirs"!

As luck (and volunteers) would have it, indeed there is a way to walk from the Pacific Ocean to the Atlantic (or vice versa).

The brainchild of the American Hiking Society and *Backpacker* magazine, the American Discovery Trail is a multiple-use trail that crosses the country from Cape Henlopen in Delaware to Point Reyes National Seashore in California. Linking rail trails, back roads, and footpaths, the trail goes through everything from cities to suburbs to farmlands to wilderness. It crosses five national scenic trails, ten national historic trails, and twenty-three national recreational trails. In many places, the trail is open to bicycles and horses in addition to walkers. It is coordinated by the American Discovery Trail Society.

This is more than a wilderness trail: It also includes urban landmarks, such as Washington, D.C.'s C&O Canal, San Francisco's Golden Gate Bridge, and the Gateway Arch in Missouri, and historic sites such as Harpers Ferry, West Virginia, Lincoln's boyhood home in Indiana, and the Pioneer Cowboy Jail in Kansas.

And of course, there are the wild places, such as Pikes Peak in Colorado and Nevada's Great Basin National Park. In fact, the trail passes through fourteen national parks and sixteen national forests. Total mileage in the system is almost 6400 miles, but that includes "extra" (nonlinear) mileage because in the Midwest, the system splits into two roughly parallel trails. Your actual thru-hiking distance depends on which fork you take. With twists, turns, climbs, and descents, figure about 4800 miles from sea to shining sea!

The only problem with the American Discovery Trail is that it isn't yet complete, so you'll need to do quite a bit of planning to chart a route in places where the route isn't yet on the ground. You can also expect a fair amount of road-walking, which can be especially rough on the feet due to the constant pounding on hard surfaces. Finally, realize that the trail does go through urban areas and the gentler country of the Midwest—so you can't expect unbroken miles of spectacular mountain scenery. Instead, you get to experience the vast range of the American landscape, from prairie to peak

The Coast-to-Coast Bar in St. Bee's celebrates England's cross-country route. The stateside version is the American Discovery Trail—and it is about twenty times as long!

and field to forest. Some people do this trail as a combination hike-bike trip.

There's another way to walk across the United States: lengthwise from Mexico to Canada. The Continental Divide and Pacific Crest Trails are very different from the American Discovery Trail because they follow major mountain chains and spend much more time in wilderness.

No matter how you cut it, a hike across America is a daunting proposition. If you like the idea of walking across a country, but don't have time for a country as big as ours, consider a couple of other options. In addition to England's Coast-to-Coast Walk, try Scotland's Southern Uplands Way (about 200 miles), or the Trans-Pyrenees Route (about 600 miles) across France and Spain. (See "Hiking Euro-style" below.)

For more information about the American Discovery Trail, visit *www.discoverytrail.org.*

National Scenic Trails.

Q. What is the difference between the national scenic trails and other long trails?

A. In 1968, Congress passed the National Trails System Act, designed to develop and protect trails that were recognized for their outstanding scenery and their important opportunities for nonmotorized recreation. Ultimately, trails included in the system were placed in three categories: national scenic

National Scenic Trails

Appalachian Trail Conference
P.O. Box 807
Harpers Ferry, WV 25425
304-535-6331
Email: info@atconf.org
www.atconf.org

Continental Divide Trail Alliance
P.O. Box 628
Pine, CO 80470
303-838-3760
Email: CDNST@aol.com
www.cdtrail.org

Continental Divide Trail Society
3704 N. Charles Street, #601
Baltimore, MD 21218-2300
410-235-9610
Email: cdtsociety@aol.com
www.cdtsociety.org

Florida Trail Association
5415 S.W. 13th Street
Gainesville, FL 32608
352-378-8823; or 877-HIKEFLA
Email: fta@florida-trail.org
www.florida-trail.org

Ice Age Park and Trail Foundation, Inc.
207 E. Buffalo Street, Suite 515
Milwaukee, WI 53202-5712
414-278-8518
Email: tracy@iceagetrail.org
www.iceagetrail.org

Natchez Trace Trail Conference, Inc.
c/o 114 N. Meadows Place
Jackson, MS 39211
601-965-0045

North Country Trail Association
229 E. Main Street
Lowell, MI 49331
888-454-NCTA
Email: hq@northcountrytrail.org
www.northcountrytrail.org

(Continued on page 35)

trails (long-distance hiking trails with outstanding scenery and natural history); national historic trails, which follow routes of historic importance and may or may not offer good hiking routes; and national recreational trails, an assortment of urban, suburban, and even wilderness trails. (The wilderness trails are usually proximate to populated areas and are much shorter than national scenic trails.)

In truth, the eight national scenic trails now included in the system make up an odd mix. Of all the national scenic trails, only the three so-called Triple Crown Trails—the Appalachian, the Pacific Crest, and the Continental Divide Trails—appear on a typical hiker's list of dream trips, and only the Appalachian and Pacific Crest Trails can be considered finished in any meaningful sense. For example, the Natchez Trace Parkway barely qualifies as a trail at all, largely following roads. The Potomac Heritage Trail is more of an idea than a trail, and although some parts of it (for example, the 187-mile C&O Canal Towpath) are certainly walkable, they are not marked as being part of a national scenic trail. Wisconsin's Ice Age Trail remains incomplete, and although it traverses stunning glacial-sculpted terrain, some of its landscape is falling victim to development. Both the North Country Trail and the Florida Trail are supported by active associations that are working to certify, complete, and mark them, but as yet there are long stretches with no marked footpath in place.

The vast majority of long-distance hikers attempt one of the Triple Crown Trails, which follow mountain ranges through some of America's most spectacular backcountry. The

Katahdin in Maine is the northern terminus of the Appalachian Trail.

Appalachian Trail draws by far the most thru-hikers: Current estimates suggest that at least 2000 people a year attempt the journey, although only a few hundred finish. The Pacific Crest Trail draws a smaller, hardier, more experienced group: Perhaps 200 people annually attempt the journey. Depending on environmental conditions, which range widely from year to year, about 50 percent finish. Only a few dozen hikers are known to have completed the Continental Divide Trail. (You'll find more about these trails later in this chapter.)

Of course, the majority of hikers who set foot on the national scenic trails do so for an hour, a day, or a

National Scenic Trails

(Continued from page 34)

Pacific Crest Trail Association
5325 Elkhorn Boulevard PMB #256
Sacramento, CA 95842
916-349-2109; or 888-PCTRAIL
Email: info@pcta.org
www.pcta.org

Potomac Trail Council
c/o AHS
1422 Fenwick Lane
Silver Spring, MD 20910
888-223-4093 x208
Email: jburke@potomactrail.org
www.potomactrail.org

The Arizona Trail is one the nation's newest long-distance hiking paths.

weekend. These trails, along with the national historic trails, the national recreation trails, and the coast-to-coast American Discovery Trail, offer Americans a wide network of paths for exploring environments from seashores to alpine tundra, from prairie to pine bog, from forest to desert.

Although some of the national scenic trails do not appeal to hikers looking for dramatic long dream trips, they all offer important recreational resources, especially to people living in nearby urban areas.

Other Longer Trails.

Q. I know about the Triple Crown Trails and the national scenic trails; where can I find information about other long trails?

A. There are dozens of long trails in the United States and Canada—not to mention in other countries. The Appalachian Long Distance Hikers

Association (*www.ALDHA.org*) has a long-trails database with basic descriptive information about long trails worldwide, along with contact information.

Some of the most popular long trails include the Colorado Trail (500 miles), the Arizona Trail (750 miles), Washington's Wonderland Trail (93 miles), Vermont's Long Trail (265 miles), and California's John Muir Trail (211 miles). Contact information for these and other long trails can be found in the regional boxes throughout this chapter.

One thing to watch for: Some long-distance trails (both in the United States and in other countries) are works-in-progress, and sometimes that progress seems slower than a sloth on a summer day. Just because a trail has a name and an enthusiastic group of volunteers doesn't mean it is ready to be hiked. In some cases, like the American section of the International Appalachian Trail, much of the trail follows roads (not everybody's favorite walking experience). Look out for phrases like "when in place, the trail will . . . " or "the route is mapped but not marked on the ground." Check the ALDHA website, read the guidebooks carefully, and call local clubs and land management agencies to find out about the current status of any long trail you plan to hike.

Volunteer Vacations.

Q. Where can I find information about volunteer vacations? What is involved in going on one of these trips?

A. Much of the construction of trails—not to mention annual maintenance, from building new water-bars to trimming vegetation—is done by volunteers. Volunteer vacations offer outdoor enthusiasts inexpensive vacations, the chance to give back to the trails community, and an opportunity to meet like-minded people and perhaps learn some new skills. All major trail clubs have volunteer opportunities, which are usually announced on their websites and in newsletters.

Many of these trips are short-term projects that last for a day or a weekend. But some organizations run trips that involve backpacking and camping out in remote (and often spectacularly beautiful) places. The Continental Divide Trail Alliance, for example, offers a variety of work trips ranging from easy hikes on gentle trails to rugged hikes at high altitudes. The American Hiking Society's volunteer vacations program (*www.americanhiking.org*) offers trips all over the country. For a small fee, participants join a crew and work on trail-maintenance projects usually for about 6 hours a day (with weekends off). Accommodations range from tent sites to cabins, depending on the location, and food is usually provided.

Avoiding Bureaucracy in National Parks.

Q. I go to the backcountry to escape crowds and lines, not to join them. I know you need permits to backpack in the national parks. But is there any way to escape the bureaucracy?

A. Admittedly, it's not a perfect system. Permits are necessary to prevent overcrowding, but the resulting bureaucratic policies range from smooth to hellish.

Many parks allow you to apply for a permit in advance, either by writing, telephone, or Internet. (Warning: National park phone-answering systems are often either busy or Byzantine.) The national parks along the Appalachian Trail and the Pacific Crest Trail have specific policies to accommodate thru-hikers arriving on foot. Precise procedures vary, so check with the park where you plan to hike, or with the trail association.

If you plan to walk in, be prepared to wait for a permit—especially in popular parks like Glacier, Yosemite, and Grand Canyon. Or, you might have a backup plan in mind—for example, choosing a less-popular trail.

In most parks, "high season" is summer. Before Memorial Day and after Labor Day far fewer people compete for permits (of course, high mountains are not usually accessible before Memorial Day), so it makes sense to hike off-season (if the weather permits).

Finally, consider avoiding the problem altogether by hiking in the national forests and wildernesses adjacent to many national parks.

National Park Alternatives

National parks can be crowded, and in some it's harder to get a permit than to cross a 3000-foot pass in a whiteout! Nearby national forests are sometimes less crowded and just as beautiful. For contact information, go to:
www.fs.fed.us/links/forests.html.

Tennessee/North Carolina: Instead of hiking in Great Smoky Mountains National Park, hike in the Pisgah National Forest along the Tennessee/North Carolina border.

Montana: Instead of hiking in Glacier National Park, hike in the Bob Marshall Wilderness.

California: Instead of hiking in Yosemite National Park, hike in the John Muir and Ansel Adams Wildernesses.

Wyoming: Instead of hiking in Yellowstone National Park, hike in the Bridger–Teton Wilderness.

Virginia: Instead of hiking in Shenandoah National Park, hike in Jefferson National Forest.

Colorado: Instead of hiking in Rocky Mountain National Park, hike in the Arapaho National Forest.

Arizona: Sorry, there's no substitute for the Grand Canyon!

Hiking with Rover.

Q. Where can I find private or public areas to go hiking with my dog, preferably in the mountains?

A. Actually, the answer is just about anywhere.

True, dogs are banned from some areas, notably many national parks and state parks, as well as many private lands. Regulations can also be strict in some urban and suburban areas. But thousands of parks, forests, and trails all over the country are open to dogs. All you have to do is choose where you'd like to hike and check with the agency that manages the land.

Not everyone is dog-friendly, however. It's your responsibility to control your pet and to make sure it doesn't ruin someone else's experience. Many wilderness rangers and land managers feel that dogs don't belong on wilderness trails because of their impact on wildlife. So if you do hike with a dog, keep it leashed. Realize that your dog's "hello" bark could terrify someone up the trail, especially if the greeting is overly exuberant. Dogs also tend to go rushing off after rabbits, deer, and other wildlife, including bears and porcupines (see Chapter 10), which is probably not a good idea. In camp, keep your dog under control, especially if you are camped near others. Never let a dog roll around in a spring where other hikers will be getting their drinking water.

Snow-free High Country.

Q. School lets out in June, and I want to get away for a couple of weeks for a backpacking trip—someplace remote and wild with big mountains. The problem is, most of the places I want to go are snowed-in until July. Where should I go? How early is too early to start?

A. Big mountains in June are always a challenge. In places like the Colorado, Wyoming, Idaho, and Montana Rockies, the Washington Cascades, the California Sierra Nevada, and other major ranges, late May into June is the height of snowmelt. Hikers who venture into the mountains will encounter ice-clogged passes up high and raging creeks and rivers down low, along with the possibility of late-spring blizzards.

You can hike in high mountains in June, but you should have solid skills. At the minimum, you should know how to use an ice ax and how to ford a river. Be aware that even lower mountains in more temperate climates can be problematic. In late May and early June, the White Mountains of New Hampshire, the Appalachian Trail in Maine, the Green Mountains of Vermont, and the Adirondacks of New York are generally accessible, but there may be lingering snow (and, I can promise you, blackflies).

So what's an alpine addict to do? Go south, of course. In June, Tennessee and North Carolina's Balds and the Smokies are in the middle of the spring wildflower bloom. Lower down, depending on the elevations, you'll see flaming azaleas and hillsides shining with rhododendron. The Southwest is another alternative. In May and June, the desert valleys are broiling, but the sky-island mountaintops are still cool and may even have lingering snow.

June decorates the southern Appalachians with wildflowers.

New Mexico's Santa Fe National Forest has miles of trails. Or try the lower elevations of the nearby Sangre de Cristo Mountains. In southern New Mexico, the Gila Wilderness is a good bet, as are Arizona's Santa Rita, Santa Catalina, and San Francisco Mountains. In southern California, the San Gabriel, San Bernardino, and San Jacinto Mountains all rise above 9000 feet.

Warning: Hiking in the Southwest can take you from simmering desert valleys to late-lying snowfields (even in June). Mountain rules apply: Be prepared for anything.

State High Points.

Q. I would like to hike to the highest point in each state. Is there a list? And is this possible?

A. Yes, there is a list. There's even a club (info on both at *www.highpointers.org*).

Climbing the majority of the fifty high points is well within the reach of most hikers—in fact, many of the state high points are within a few yards of a parking area! Even when a state high point is a bona fide mountain, it's not necessarily the most difficult climb in that state. For example, Colorado boasts many peaks with full-fledged climbing challenges, but its high point is 14,433-foot Mount Elbert, a gentle giant of a mountain whose summit can be reached by day hikers. Similarly, California's 14,494-foot Mount Whitney presents no technical challenges. It's simply a very long walk up a very big hill!

Denali (otherwise known as Mount McKinley) is the highest peak in North America. Climbing it requires mountaineering experience and a high level of fitness.

But four of the peaks on the list are true mountaineering challenges that lay down the gauntlet: The high points of Alaska (Denali, 20,320 feet), Wyoming (Gannett Peak, 13,804 feet), Montana (Granite Peak, 12,799 feet), and Washington (Mount Rainier, 14,410 feet) are major endeavors, requiring enormous endurance, technical skills, and equipment. Climbing Denali, in particular, is a full-fledged expedition; many climbing parties "practice" for Himalayan climbs on this dangerous, unpredictable peak. You will probably need to join a commercial expedition with professional guides to attempt to climb Denali. As for fitness, you should be in shape to run a marathon (or do an equivalent feat in one day). Gannet, Granite, and Rainier aren't nearly as difficult and dangerous as Denali—all three can be climbed by novices if they go with experienced guides. But that doesn't make them easy.

Peak-Bagging.

Q. I'm looking for a real outdoor challenge; I want to beef up my skills and really test myself. Trouble is, I live in Connecticut. Where can I go?

A. If you're up for a long-term challenge, check out the Four Thousand Footer Club, which recognizes hikers who have climbed the highest peaks in New England. Today, the club maintains three lists of peaks and those who have climbed them: the White Mountain Four Thousand Footers, the New England Four Thousand Footers, and the New England Hundred Highest. If that's not enough challenge for you, the club also recognizes those who have climbed the mountains on these lists in winter. Contact Eugene Daniel III, secretary, Four Thousand Footer Committee, 42 Eastman Street, Concord, NH 03301.

Similarly, the Adirondack 46ers Club recognizes those who have summited the forty-six highest peaks in New York's Adirondack range: *www.adk46r.org*.

Those who live in the West and are looking for a similar challenge can check out the fifty-four peaks in Colorado that rise to elevations of more than 14,000 feet: *www.coloradofourteeners.org*.

For Southerners, there's the South Beyond 6000 Club. Contact the Carolina Mountain Club (Box 68, Asheville, NC 28802; *www.carolinamtnclub.com*) for information on the forty peaks, mostly in North Carolina, that rise above 6000 feet.

Eastern Trails

Why the Appalachian Trail?

Q. Why is it that the Appalachian Trail is so popular and gets so much press? As a Westerner who grew up in the Rocky Mountains, I just don't get it!

A. Longevity probably has something to do with it. Although the Appalachian Trail and the Pacific Crest Trail were conceived in the same decade, the Appalachian Trail got off to a faster start. The AT was proposed in 1921 by a regional planner named Benton MacKaye, who would later go on to help found the Wilderness Society. Committed and energetic volunteers (like the indefatigable organizer and trail builder Myron Avery) took up the project with the support of the Appalachian Trail Conference, which was formed to coordinate the work of local trail clubs. The availability of good guidebooks and the high quality of trail maintenance also attracted hikers—as did the fact that the trail is readily accessible to so many major population centers. The shelter system, a well-marked path, the temperate climate, and the fact that much of the trail can be hiked year-round all serve to make the AT an inviting destination.

I understand your confusion: Although it does have some beautiful mountain scenery, the AT doesn't hold a candle to the big Western mountain trails. But many Westerners have told me that they hike the AT for its lush greenness and its beauty in spring and fall.

The thru-hiker culture also contributes to the AT mystique. Certainly, the dream of a six-month thru-hike has captured the public's imagination.

The traveling community of this unique American pilgrimage has given the AT traditions, lore, and a whole culture that are found nowhere else. The intersection of the hiking community with small Appalachian towns is another unique factor. In a very real sense, a thru-hike of the Appalachian Trail is a personal pilgrimage, a wilderness experience, and a journey of discovery of quintessential small-town rural America.

A Short Hike on the AT.

Q. What part of the Appalachian Trial is best for two guys looking for a 5–7-day trip? We are looking for a moderately strenuous trip with great scenery and large mountains, and we can go anytime between March and October.

A. The AT's biggest mountains are found on its northern and southern ends. In the middle, the elevations drop.

Spring and fall are the ideal times to hike the southern Appalachians, from Georgia through Virginia. Springtime brings bowers of rhododendron,

Katahdin—the "greatest mountain" in Maine—lies just north of Maine's so-called 100-mile Wilderness, which offers a beautiful week-long backpacking route.

Wild ponies are one of the attractions in southern Virginia's Mount Rogers National Recreation Area, home of Virginia's highest peak.

beautiful flame azaleas, and mountain laurel. Key big mountains in the South include the Great Smoky Mountains, the Tennessee–North Carolina Balds (in the Hot Springs–Erwin area), and the Mount Rogers National Recreation Area in Virginia, where you can climb to the state's high point and see wild ponies. All of these mountains impart the feeling of the much bigger mountains out West, perhaps because many of them don't have trees on top. Views are open and the skies are big.

In summer, I'd head north to avoid the heat. The White Mountains of New Hampshire offer an arctic-alpine wonderland (bring warm clothes and good raingear), and all of Maine is spectacular. These mountains are also glorious in fall foliage. Autumn weather can turn fierce and cold, so you would need extra gear. One of my favorite peaks in Maine is Saddleback; West Mountain and Avery Peak also offer beautiful views; and, of course, Katahdin, where the AT ends, deserves its Abenaki name "greatest mountain."

As for strenuous, I'd be willing to bet you'd agree that any of these are moderately strenuous (at least). The Mount Rogers Recreation Area is the easiest; western Maine is the toughest. Call the Appalachian Trail Conference for more info.

Beyond the Appalachian Trail.

Q. All I seem to read about is the Appalachian Trail. What about other East Coast trails?

A. Though the temperate forested East Coast environment is fairly homogeneous, compared with the vast variations in the West, it offers a surprising amount of variety, ranging from an extensive trails network in New Hampshire's White Mountains, to an interlocking system of long trails in Pennsylvania, to the subtropical lowlands of the Florida Trail.

Don't expect all East Coast trails to be as well marked or maintained as the Appalachian Trail. Many are—but others don't have the army of volunteers needed to maintain them. Some trails have shelter systems, but many do not. The accompanying boxes list a variety of Eastern Trails that should keep you hiking for years to come.

Mount Washington in Winter?

Q. A friend asked me to hike New Hampshire's Mount Washington in January. We have only car-camped before. Is this crazy? What gear do we need?

A. Yes, it's crazy. Commit your friend to an asylum immediately. Commit yourself, too, if you actually consider this seriously. Not because Mount Washington in winter is impossible (it's not). It is, however, seriously dangerous for inexperienced (and even experienced) hikers.

People *die* up there. They die up there every year—in August, let alone January. I've hiked 17,000 miles in the last 12 years, I've done some mountaineering, and I've slept out for a week when it was 30 below zero. But I wouldn't go near the Whites in January without major expedition equipment and three other people who I knew had top-notch winter backpacking

Northeastern Parks & Trails

▲ Adirondack State Park, New York. www.adk.org

▲ Baxter State Park, Maine. www.mainerec.com/baxter1.html

▲ C&O Canal Towpath, Washington, D.C. and Maryland. www.canal.com

▲ Cohos Trail, New Hampshire. www.cohostrail.org

▲ Finger Lakes Trail, New York. www.fingerlakes.net/trailsystem

▲ International Appalachian Trail, Maine and Quebec. www.internationalat.org

▲ Long Path, New York. www.nynjtc.org/trails/longpath/index.html

▲ Long Trail, Vermont. www.greenmountainclub.org

▲ Northville–Lake Placid Trail, New York. www.adk.org

▲ Pennsylvania Trails. www.kta-hike.org

▲ Tuscarora–Big Blue Trail, Virginia and Pennsylvania. www.patc.net/hiking/destinations/tuscarora/

▲ White Mountain National Forest, New Hampshire. www.fs.fed.us/r9/white/

experience. The winter Whites is no place for novices. It's not even a place for intermediates.

But that's no reason not to go winter camping! It's a wonderful way to experience nature, if you have the right gear and skills, which you can develop with practice in less dangerous conditions. You don't have to go far from home to have an adventure. Even your tame, boring, old local park will seem different in a winter white-out.

So, where go? Other Eastern winter options for beginners:

Check out the Northville–Lake Placid Trail in New York's Adirondack Mountains, the Black Forest Trail in Pennsylvania, or the Appalachian Trail in Shenandoah National Park in Virginia. The Northville–Lake Placid Trail and the AT both have shelters, which gives you an added margin of safety. The Northville–Lake Placid route is a lowland route that stays below tree line, is relatively flat, and has lovely lakeside campsites. The Black Forest Trail in Pennsylvania features more ups-and-downs for a challenging workout. The AT in Shenandoah runs the ridge and has some good open views. The southern latitude ameliorates the effect of the high elevations; this is where you'll get a true mountain hiking feeling, without the risks of the Whites.

Western Destinations

How Hard Is the Pacific Crest Trail?

Q. I'm thinking about hiking the Pacific Crest Trail. Can an inexperienced hiker handle a long-distance trail like the PCT? How rigorous is it?

A. I have to confess I found it rigorous.

Here's what you'll encounter: Elevations range from near sea-level on the Oregon–Washington border to 13,200 feet atop Forester Pass in the High Sierra. In the desert valleys of southern California, you'll find desert daytime temperatures in the 100s (once, my thermometer told us that it was 118 in the shade!). You may also have to carry a lot of water, because water sources are few and far between. (We occasionally had to carry as much as 6 liters a person, although that is the exception, not the rule; see Chapter 5, "How Much Water?")

Then, just as soon as you think you'll never see enough water again in your life, you enter the High Sierra, where water (in either flowing or frozen form) rules. You'll most likely need an ice ax to cross late-lingering snowfields that block the trail. (So you'll need a map and compass, too.) You'll also need steady nerves to cross snowmelt-swollen streams in the valleys between the ice-choked high passes. Because of the PCT's challenges, inexperienced hikers should plan a few shorter trips first to learn how to deal with high mountains, deserts, and snow travel.

The good news is that the trail is well graded and in excellent condition. Good maps and guidebooks are available. The scenery is phenomenal, and you'll walk through six out of North America's seven ecozones, seeing everything from cactus to limber pine, rattlesnakes to black bears. This really is the trip of a lifetime. If you're committed to the idea (see "Thru-hiking à Deux," Chapter 7) and in reasonable shape, go for it! You won't be disappointed.

California Parks & Trails

- ▲ California Coast Trail. www.californiacoastaltrail.org/
- ▲ High Sierra Trail www.sierrawilderness.com/seki.html.tahoerimtrail.org
- ▲ John Muir Trail. www.pcta.org/jmt/index.html
- ▲ Lassen Volcanic National Park. www.nps.gov/lavo
- ▲ Sequoia–Kings Canyon National Parks. www.nps.gov/seki
- ▲ Shasta–Trinity National Forest. www.r5.fs.fed.us/shastatrinity/
- ▲ Tahoe Rim Trail. www.tahoerimtrail.org/
- ▲ Tahoe–Yosemite Trail. www.thebackpacker.com/trails/ca/trail_452.php
- ▲ Yosemite National Park. www.nps.gov/yose

Snow-free Sierra.

Q. We're avid campers in fair physical condition, living in southern California. We were hoping to do the High Sierra Trail. How early can we start? We're after an easygoing, eye-popping, get-me-out-of-the-city trip—but we don't want to deal with snow and ice.

A. In anything that even resembles a normal snow year in the Sierra, you should be home-free by the second week of July. You can't beat the High Sierra for the kind of scenery you're looking for. It's certainly one of the most beautiful trails I've ever seen—and a good alternative to the more crowded John Muir Trail (see below).

The Sierra snowmelt is mostly an impediment in mid- and late June, when ice axes and the ability to self-arrest are requirements for those trying

In mid-summer, snow is not usually a problem in the High Sierra, even at 12,000-foot Muir Pass.

to cross the high passes. In heavier snow years, the white stuff can certainly stick around well into mid-July, but by late July the trails are fairly dry even in the snowiest years. Of course, it's always a good idea to get up-to-date information about conditions from the ranger station just before you go.

The John Muir Trail.

Q. I keep hearing about the John Muir Trail. Does it live up to its reputation? And where can I get detailed info?

A. Running the length of California's High Sierra, the JMT routinely shows up on the cover of gear catalogs and outdoor magazines, and in "best of" lists by hikers and outdoor writers. I agree, the glaciated terrain offers some of the most impressive mountain scenery to be found anywhere in the United States or otherwise. It's also an extremely remote, big wilderness. Frequently, on the trail, you'll find yourself just stopping to stare while your mind tries to take it all in.

Some facts: The John Muir Trail runs 212 miles from the summit of 14,494-foot Mount Whitney (the highest peak in the contiguous United States) to Yosemite Valley in Yosemite National Park. Along the way, it crosses eight high passes, including Forester Pass, which at 13,180 feet is also the highest point on the Pacific Crest Trail. The JMT also goes through Sequoia and Kings Canyon National Parks, the John Muir and Ansel Adams Wildernesses, and Devil's Postpile National Monument. The JMT is contiguous with the Pacific Crest Trail for most of its route.

A couple of practicalities: The main hiking season is mid-July through September. Permits are required and can be difficult to get in the midsummer hiking season. You can expect to encounter a lot of company—both human and ursine. To avoid both the other backpackers and the bears, you might consider camping a short distance away from popular campsites along lakes and streams. Also be sure to take appropriate bear precautions: If you camp in the well-used sites, use the metal food-storage lockers (bear boxes) provided for that purpose. If you camp away from food-storage lockers, be sure you're carrying bear-proof food storage containers; these are portable bear-proof canisters, which are available commercially or from the national park office (see "Bear Canisters," Chapter 10).

For more on the JMT, see "Mountain Mileage" (Chapter 5).

This view from the west side of Mount Whitney is typical of the mountains Ansel Adams dubbed the "range of light."

Climbing Mount Hood.

Q. I will be visiting Portland, Oregon, and would like to climb Mount Hood. Although I exercise regularly and the motivation is there, I do not have a lot of serious hiking experience. What would be the best strategy for climbing in terms of mileage? Also, I was thinking about the possibility of an overnight. What wildlife might we encounter, and what precautions should we take? Also, what can we expect in terms of weather so that we can dress accordingly?

A. If you hang around Mount Hood for long, you'll inevitably hear the story of "a lady climbing Mount Hood in high-heeled shoes and a dress." Mount Hood is the most frequently climbed snowcapped mountain in America, and in the nineteenth century some stalwart women were indeed known to have reached the summit in flowing dresses. Nonetheless, despite its accessibility, Mount Hood is still a major peak that should not be underestimated. It is subject to rockfall and violent storms, even in summer. Without significant high-mountain experience, you may not be able to pick out a safe route or assess the changes of dangerous conditions. It's not an especially difficult climb, but it is potentially dangerous, even deadly.

Given what you've told me about your background, I wouldn't advise a climb of Mount Hood without a guide. Guide service is available from several schools/concessionaires. Mount Hood National Forest can provide recommendations (503-622-7674). With a guide service and moderate luck with the weather, anyone in good shape has a shot at the top.

A beautiful alternative would be to explore the timberline area of Mount Hood by following the Pacific Crest Trail from Timberline Lodge. Timberline Lodge was built in the 1930s as a WPA project. It's a prime example of the "parkitecture" style of backcountry lodges, which features artisan workmanship of wood, iron, and glass. And it offers gourmet cuisine, too.

Pacific Northwest Parks & Trails

▲ Deschutes and Ochoco National Forests, Oregon. www.fs.fed.us/r6/centraloregon/index.html
▲ Mount Adams, Washington. www.fs.fed.us/gpnf/wilderness/wi_mta.htm
▲ Mount Baker–Snoqualmie National Forest, Washington. www.fs.fed.us/r6/mbs/index.html
▲ Mount Hood, Oregon. www.fs.fed.us/r6/mthood/
▲ Mount Rainier National Park, Washington. www.nps.gov/mora
▲ North Cascades National Park, Washington. www.nps.gov/noca
▲ Olympic National Park, Washington. www.nps.gov/olym
▲ Pacific Northwest Trail, Montana, Idaho, Washington. www.pnt.org
▲ Wonderland Trail, Washington. www.nps.gov/mora/trail/wonder.htm

From the lodge, you can hike north around the western flank of the mountain. The Timberline Trail circles Mount Hood in its entirety. The entire Timberline Trail takes a few days, but you could always do an out-and-back hike, perhaps camping overnight.

As far as gear is concerned, if you stay at the timberline (around 6000 feet) in midsummer, you should have two light warm layers (a polypro and a light fleece) for your torso and one warm layer for your legs. You should also have good raingear (pants and jacket). If you climb the mountain, you'll need additional warm layers for both legs and torso; also gloves, hat, ice ax, and gaiters. The climbing service will provide a list of required gear.

Mount Rainier: Up or Over?

Q. I'm going to be vacationing near Seattle and want to get in some strenuous hiking. I've been thinking about taking on Mount Rainier, but I can't decide whether to go up or around. How hard is the Wonderland Trail? How hard is the climb?

A. Both are considered difficult trips, but for very different reasons. And they are so different that if you didn't have a constant view of Mount Rainier towering above, you might start to wonder if you were on the same mountain.

The Wonderland Trail is a 93-mile loop trail that circles the mountain. The park service recommends that you take about 14 days for the entire trip, which gives you plenty of time to cover the mileage and do a little exploring.

The climb requires that you be in peak physical condition. Many hikers rate this climb as one of the most difficult things they've ever done. I've heard people compare it to marathons and triathlons, and it is often called the most arduous endurance climb in the lower forty-eight states. Personally, I thought it was much tougher than climbing the much higher (19,340-foot) Mount Kilimanjaro in Africa. Only about half of the approximately 12,000 people who attempt the climb each year succeed.

If you're not an experienced climber, you should sign on for a climb with the Park's concession guide service. You'll be required to take a 1-day mountaineering skills class, which covers the basics of ice ax use, crampon techniques, self-arrest, and rope handling. The climb itself is a 2-day affair. On day one, you'll hike from Paradise (about 5000 feet) to Muir Camp (at about 10,000 feet), where you'll spend the night. Guides will wake you up in the middle of the night—precisely when depends on the weather—and you'll suit up and start climbing. The climb doesn't require technical skills, but you will have to do some fancy footwork on a rock rib, as well as some steep cramponing, and take a few hops across narrow crevasses. You'll be roped in small groups and expected to keep up with the person in front of you. Ideally, you reach the 14,410-foot summit at sunrise, to revel in the view (south to Mount Hood, north into Canada). Then you turn around and go all the way down, 9000 long steep feet, to Paradise. It's an absolutely exhausting day.

Which is better? It depends on what you prefer: Circles or straight lines? One big climb or several little ones? (Your total elevation gain on the Wonderland Trail will actually be more than twice the elevation gain of going to the summit!) Walking alone or climbing in a group? The infinite variety of the tree line or the stark purity of rock and ice?

Perhaps it's not an either-or choice, but merely a decision of which to do first. Note: The optimum hiking and climbing season runs from late July through August.

The Southwest in Winter.

Q. I'm planning a trip to Arizona and California this winter. I would like to do a couple of weeklong hikes. Any places you can recommend?

A. The Southwest is a great winter destination for cabin fever–crazed hikers.

I hiked about 400 miles of the Arizona Trail in December and January, and it was one of the best hikes I ever did. Almost all of the nearly 800-mile-long trail can be hiked in winter, although you might be trudging in snow at the higher elevations. Don't complain! You can melt snow, and that solves one of the great problems of hiking in the Southwest: finding enough water. The Arizona Trail goes through the Coronado National Forest, which includes the Huachuca, Santa Rita, and Santa Catalina Mountains (all beautiful in winter), parts of Saguaro National Park, the Superstition and Mazatzal Wilder-

Snowfall on yucca: It's rare, but it does snow in the Southwest.

nesses, the Coconino National Forest, and the San Francisco Mountains, as well as the Kaibab National Forest and the Grand Canyon. You'll have no trouble at all keeping busy for two weeks!

The Grand Canyon in winter is also spectacular—and not very crowded. You have to go in from the South Rim because the North Rim roads close in winter. As you drop lower and lower, the temperatures get warmer and warmer; you may even find yourself hiking in shorts!

Southern California also offers some winter hiking possibilities. However, many of the trails go into higher mountain ranges, which can be snow-covered. You'll have to check conditions before you go, or stay at lower elevations. Some places to check: the Cleveland National Forest, the San Bernardino National Forest (which includes the San Jacinto Wilderness), the Angeles National Forest, and Anza-Borrego Desert State Park, which contains 600,000 acres, making it California's largest state park.

Can I Handle the "Grand"?

Q. I'm 54 and not in great shape. I would like to plan a trip to the Grand Canyon with a friend. Are there novice-to-intermediate hiking trails there?

A. You bet there are—although you'll enjoy them more if you at least make an attempt to get in shape first. The Bright Angel and South Kaibab Trails go from the South Rim down to Bright Angel Campground and Phantom Ranch; the North Kaibab Trail goes up the North Rim. These trails are practically highways, suitable for mule traffic and tourists wearing the most ridiculous footwear imaginable (although I recommend sturdy shoes or boots). Canyon rangers suggest that first-time visitors get their introductory taste of the Canyon on one of these so-called corridor trails. On your return visit (and I'm betting you'll want to return) you can graduate to some of the more remote trails, which require map and compass skills, a little bit of rock scrambling, and heavier-duty footwear.

Despite the easy footway of the corridor trails, there are still some challenges unique to the Grand Canyon that you shouldn't underestimate.

First, there's the issue of water. There's very little water in the Canyon (and very little shade, either). Don't judge the temperature by the weather on the rim. As you descend, the temperature climbs 3 to 5 degrees (and sometimes more) per 1000 feet. That means that when it's a comfortable 70 degrees on the rim, it can be in the 90s down below. So you need to take a lot of water.

The second challenge for day hikers, especially for novices, is judging when to turn around. The problem with *any* canyon is that you start by going downhill. Downhill is easy on the well-graded corridor trails, and you may not realize that for every mile you go down, it's probably going to take about twice as long to come back up. You'll definitely want to pace yourself so that you have plenty of time and water to retrace your steps. Decide how long you want to hike, then turn around when you've used up one-third of your time (or one-third of your water, whichever comes first).

Downhill hiking also places stress on your feet. Be sure you have broken in your boots before the hike, and be sure that your toes don't jam up against the front of the boot. Carry blister treatment and know how to use it.

If you're planning on actually camping in the Canyon, you have a couple of options.

From the South Rim, a lot of people go all the way down the South Kaibab Trail in one day, then camp at Bright Angel Creek or stay at Phantom Ranch (reservations for both are required and should be made well in advance; phone numbers for all Canyon lodges are available at the park's website). Coming up from the River, you would take the Bright Angel Trail because that allows you to divide the ascent and stop overnight at Indian Gardens Campground. Most people in average shape can handle this *if* they give themselves plenty of time, avoid walking in the heat of the day, and take plenty of water.

Similarly, if you're hiking from the more remote North Rim, you'd want to split up the hike and camp overnight at Cottonwood Campground. Because the North Kaibab Trail is 14 miles (considerably longer than the Bright Angel or South Kaibab Trails), you might want to break up the hike both going down and going up. Additionally, some people travel Rim-to-Rim, going down one side of the Canyon and coming up the other. However, this requires some fancy shuttling of vehicles.

Any way you hike the Canyon, I'm betting that it'll be a highlight!

Continental Divide.

Q. How is the Continental Divide Trail different from the Pacific Crest Trail?

A. The two Western mountain trails share many similarities, including a wide range of environments, magnificent scenery, and physical challenge. Both require solid backcountry skills and the ability to cover high mileage because of the short snow-free hiking season in high mountains.

At this time, one of the major differences is that the Continental Divide is not yet complete. So CDT hikers must be able to chart a route where the footpath is not yet on the ground, and then use navigation skills—map, compass, and possibly a global positioning system (GPS) device—to find their way.

Another difference is that while the PCT largely stays in remote wilderness areas where the primary land use is recreation, the CDT spends more time in multiple-use lands. You'll see a lot more grazing and logging on the CDT than you will on the PCT. You'll also sometimes have to share the trail with bicycles and motorized vehicles.

Finally, the CDT offers an added dimension: The Continental Divide is a landscape full of history. Hikers walk in the steps of Indian traders, mountain men and fur traders, miners, railroad builders, and settlers. *Where the Waters Divide*, a book I co-authored with my husband Dan Smith, describes a thru-hike of this wild and remote long-distance trail.

The Continental Divide Trail goes through some of North America's wildest country, including Montana's Bob Marshall Wilderness.

A late afternoon thunderstorm gathers in Colorado's San Juan Mountains.

Colorado Thunder.

Q. I've heard that thunderstorms on the Colorado Trail are a major hazard. Is this true?

A. Thunderstorms are a hazard in many mountains on a summer afternoon. But you're right. Some mountains seem to be storm magnets, and certainly one of the most impressive and frightening natural spectacles I've ever seen is a purple thundercloud flying across the Colorado sky—right at me.

Actually, the builders of the Colorado Trail took this into account when designing the route. The Colorado Trail was conceived as a recreational resource for hikers of average ability and experience. In some sections, much of the trail is below tree line, rising into the tundra to cross a pass, then descending back into the safety of the forest. The ups and downs sometimes make for frustrating hiking, especially for backpackers who crave dramatic scenery, but the route is undoubtedly safer as a result.

That said, the Colorado Trail inevitably boasts many sections of above–tree line travel where there is no shelter for miles at a time. As in any mountains where afternoon storms are common, it's wise to try to plan your days so that you are off the exposed ridges by mid-afternoon, when storms are most common. In addition to the guidebooks, it's a good idea to bring a Forest Service map so that you can bail out if necessary on a side trail. For more on lightning, see Chapter 9.

Midwestern Destinations

Q. Help! I love the outdoors, especially mountains, but I live in Chicago. Where do I go to hike without having to get on a plane?

A. Well, there's always Chicago's Sears Tower.

As far as truly big mountains go, you're out of luck. Even getting to little mountains requires a looooong drive either to the Porcupine Mountains of Michigan's Upper Peninsula, or the Ozarks of Missouri and Arkansas.

Although the Midwest is a pauper in the mountain department, it does boast some lovely scenery, especially along the Great Lakes. Two national scenic trails cross parts of the Midwest: the North Country Trail, which runs from New York to North Dakota, and the Ice Age Trail in Wisconsin. The Buckeye Trail loops around the state of Ohio, and the Ozarks boast two long trails in Missouri and Arkansas.

Other features of the Midwestern outdoors are tallgrass prairies and national wildlife refuges, where birders can add to their life lists.

Rocky Mountain Parks & Trails

▲ Bob Marshall Wilderness Complex, Montana. *www.fs.fed.us/r1/flathead/wilderness/Wilderness.htm*
▲ Bridger–Teton National Forest, Wyoming. *www.fs.fed.us/btnf/welcome.htm*
▲ Colorado Trail, Colorado. *www.coloradotrail.org*
▲ Glacier National Park, Montana. *www.nps.gov/glac*
▲ Grand Teton National Park, Wyoming. *www.nps.gov/grte*
▲ Rocky Mountain National Park, Colorado. *www.nps/romo*
▲ San Juan National Forest, Colorado. *www.fs.fed.us/r2/sanjuan/*
▲ Yellowstone National Park, Wyoming. *www.nps.gov/yell*

Midwestern Destinations

▲ Isle Royale National Park, Michigan. *www.nps.gov/isro*
▲ Indiana Dunes National Lakeshore, Indiana. *www.nps.gov.indu*
▲ Ozark Highlands Trail, Arkansas. *www.hikearkansas.com*
▲ Ozark Trail, Missouri. *www.confedmo.com/ozktrltm.htm*
▲ Porcupine Mountains State Park, Michigan. *www.ring.com/travel/porkies.htm#trails*
▲ Buckeye Trail, Ohio. *www.buckeyetrail.org*
▲ Door County State Parks, Wisconsin. *www.dnr.state.wi.us/org/land/parks/specific/peninsula/DCparks.htm*
▲ Superior Hiking Trail, Minnesota. *www.shta.org*
▲ Ouachita Trail, Oklahoma and Arkansas. *www.fs.fed.us/oonf/rec/onrt.htm*
▲ Sheltowee Trace, Kentucky. *www.gorp.com/gorp/resource/us_trail/ky/sheltowe.htm*

Day hiking paths in Greece follow trading and farming routes that date back thousands of years.

Hiking Abroad

Hiking Euro-style.

Q. I've done a lot of hiking in the United States, and I'm thinking of trying one of the European long trails. Where do I get information? How are they similar to or different from American trails?

A. A vast network of long trails criss-crosses the European continent. Like trails in America, they exist in various degrees of completion. Some are well marked, some are barely marked at all. Some have status as "national trails"; others are cobbled together by local groups. France and England have particularly well-developed systems of long trails. As in America, trails are marked in a variety of ways. Most common are colored paint blazes. You'll see red and white stripes, yellow circles, green triangles—sometimes all at the same time, painted in a bewildering, polychromatic array on a signpost or a tree.

One difference between European hiking and American hiking is that Europeans are more likely to sleep indoors, either in hiker hostels, B&Bs, small inns, or high-country refuges. Wild camping, as it's called, is the exception rather than the rule.

Another difference is that Europe has much less true wilderness than the United States. You'll rarely hike for more than a few miles without seeing some signs of human history, habitation, or cultivation. This makes for an interesting cultural experience, but if you're the type of backpacker who likes to spend days without so much as another hiker in sight, it may not be your cup of tea.

Speaking of tea, the U.K.–based Ramblers Association *(www.ramblers. org.uk/info/paths/paths.html)* maintains a website with links to information on dozens of European walking routes, including England's system of national trails, including Scotland's Southern Upland Way and England's Pennine Way. The European Rambler's Association *(www.era-ewv-ferp.org)* additionally provides information on the so-called E trails, Europe's equivalent of America's national scenic trails system with tens of thousands of kilometers from Greece to Scotland and from Spain to Sweden. While many of the websites of European trail organizations are in European languages, English guidebooks are often available. The best place to start is the Adventurous Traveler Bookstore *(www.AdventurousTraveler.com)*.

Third-World Hiking.

Q. I'm interested in trekking in Asia, Africa, and South America. Do I need a guide? How is hiking in a developing country different than hiking in the United States?

A. Whether or not you need the services of a guide depends on your skills and comfort level (the most important skill being your ability to find your way, even if you only have a poor map). It also depends on where you're hiking. In some places, the government or park management will require that you use guides. In places that attract large numbers of tourists-trekkers-climbers (like Nepal's Himalayas, Mount Kilimanjaro in Africa, or the Inca Trail in Peru) a whole economic culture has grown up around servicing visitors. In other places, environmentalists are trying to save natural resources by bringing in ecotourism, but such tourism needs to economically benefit local people to be sustainable. Hiring porters and guides may not be required, but your willingness to pay a few dollars a day is greatly appreciated by the very poor people who provide these services, and it is a contribution you can make to the ultimate sustainability of these worthwhile environmental projects. You can arrange for guides in advance through U.S.–based travel companies, but you can also make arrangements much less expensively when you get to where you're going.

In developing countries, you'll find that, except in national parks primarily visited by tourists, the trekking routes are often traditional paths used by people to get from one place to another. Trekking is therefore as much a cultural experience as an outdoor experience; it is not, technically speaking, a wilderness experience. Often, you'll stay in modest local lodgings at night and eat local food.

The biggest hiking concern (assuming you're hiking in a region that is politically stable) is probably water. Water in developing nations—even in

Porters in Nepal carry heavy loads. Many depend on tourists to support their families.

pure-looking high mountains—must be treated, preferably with a purifier that kills viruses and removes *Giardia lamblia* and other waterborne microbes (see Chapter 9).

Two other issues to consider when planning a hiking trip in third world countries: First is personal health and safety. Before you go, check with the United States Department of State *(www.state.gov)* for travel advisories and warnings. Political turmoil and disease outbreaks are as mobile as a traveling salesman. Be sure your "standard" inoculations (like tetanus, measles, mumps, and rubella) are up-to-date, and get the latest recommendations for other inoculations from your doctor or the Centers for Disease Control *(www.cdc. gov/travel/reference.htm)*.

The second issue is communication. English-speaking guides can interpret the culture for you and help keep you out of trouble, but before you go, make the effort to learn fifty to a hundred words. (Some trekking guidebooks, like those for Nepal and Tibet published by The Mountaineers Books, have glossaries.) A linguist friend once told me that six hundred words and a basic grasp of language structure makes you functional. It seems like a small investment of time for a large benefit. You'll reap a lot of smiles when you attempt to say "I hold your feet" *(Skikamoo, mzee)* in Swahili, the polite greeting given to an older person, or "I salute the God within you" *(Namaste),* a traditional greeting in Nepal.

Where in the World?

Q. Say you had just one opportunity to do a big trip and you were looking for the most variety and great scenery. Where would you go?

A. The only way to answer this question is with the disclaimer that the world is full of spectacular places to backpack (and I haven't been to *all* of them . . . yet).

Adventure travel is one of those things you can't "try before you buy." But if we're going to spend our hard-earned vacation time and money on one "big trip," we want some assurance that we're making the right decision.

There are many destinations I'd recommend with caveats:

▲ Nepal, if you are interested in the third world. (Warning: check the current political situation, which has been unstable in recent years.)
▲ East Africa's volcanoes, if you want to climb.
▲ France's Grandes Randonnées System, if you can handle the language challenge.
▲ Peru's Inca Trail, if you don't freak out at signs of political instability.
▲ England's Coast-to-Coast, if you don't mind hiking in populated areas.

But to recommend a destination without any of these reservations, I'd choose New Zealand. I'd pick New Zealand not only because that's the place I'd go back to if I could only do one more big trip, but because almost everyone I've ever met who has been there says exactly the same thing. The world, it seems, is divided into two kinds of people: those who have visited New Zealand and want to go back, and those who haven't been there yet.

New Zealand boasts terrain ranging from active volcanoes to rain forest to alpine peaks to Mediterranean coastline so beautiful you'd swear you were walking through a travel poster. A system of "Great Walks" features the

A spectacular location for a refuge in the French Alps

country's hiking highlights. In addition, there are more than nine hundred backcountry huts on trails and in parks throughout the country.

New Zealand is an easy country for hikers to travel in. It's English-speaking and politically stable. With a population of just over three million, it has thousands of square miles of protected backcountry and parks. It's also inexpensive, with scores of backpacker inns that cater to outdoor recreationists. Outdoor retailers are plentiful, so you can buy supplies like camping gas. The Department of Conservation (the Kiwi equivalent of our National Park Service) is friendly, informative, and helpful. Some public buses even schedule stops at trailheads and Department of Conservation offices. (One driver of a bus I was on carried binoculars so he could look up the mountain to see if he should wait for any straggling hikers! Now *that's* a country that's friendly to backpackers!) And if you want to take a break from backpacking, there are dozens of other outdoor activities available, from sea-kayaking to bungee-jumping.

There are only two disadvantages that I can think of: the strong southern sun (if you have fair skin, you'll need to use gobs of sunscreen and wear a hat, and perhaps long pants and long-sleeved shirts); and the sand flies, which are New Zealand's answer to Scottish midges, Alaskan mosquitoes, and Maine blackflies. Carry an insect repellent that contains DEET (it'll be marked on the label).

For more information, visit *www.doc.govt.nz.*

Chapter 3

Food
SATISFYING MEALS THAT TRAVEL WELL

alk about scenery all you want. Wax euphoric about getting in touch with nature. But we all know what *really* gets to a hiker's heart: good grub at the end of a grueling grunt. Hikers eat everything that doesn't run away. We love trading recipes and advice. Food questions range from the simple (how much food does a hiker eat?) to the complicated (what about making a *really* good meal in the backcountry?).

Backcountry Cup o' Joe.

Q. I have been charged with making "campsite coffee" for our next hike. Instant is out of the question. I've heard rumblings about boiling the coffee grounds, but I don't know how to do it. We (there are four guys) are attempting to impress our girlfriends with a special meal. Please help!

A. At your service—anything to help romance bloom in the wild outdoors.

Really, the easiest way to make real coffee is to simply make real coffee. Get one of those filter baskets—the kind that uses a metal mesh rather than a paper filter (less trash to worry about). You could even pre-grind your favorite beans before the trip. Then all you have to do is boil water and run it though the coffee into a water bottle set aside for that purpose. Even easier, you could use coffee bags (they work like tea bags and produce a decent, if not quite connoisseur-quality cup of coffee).

However, you guys are trying to *impress*, so why go the easy route?

First things first. Are your fair lasses going to be wowed with up-to-the-minute gadgetry and elegant savoir-faire? Or are they more interested in macho-types who whack down trees with a single swipe of their Swiss army knives?

If the former, get thee to an outfitter, where the folks dedicated to inventing ever more ways for us poor backpackers to turn ounces into pounds have found the solution to all your gourmet problems. A portable espresso maker? Several models available. A backcountry stainless-steel lightweight percolator? Certainly, sir: Would you like it to serve two or four?

But if you suspect your girlfriend secretly craves that you turn into a backwoods he-man, good ole cowboy coffee is the only way to go. Build up the fire (in a suitable minimum-impact sort of way, in an area that won't be adversely affected, and always using preexisting fire-rings, of course; macho ain't what it used to be). Throw on the pot, boil the water, toss in the grounds. If you're the measuring type, use the same proportions as you would in making regular coffee—about 2 tablespoons of coffee for every 6 ounces of water.

Let it sit for a bit, then pour in a dollop of cold water and tap on the pot, supposedly to settle the grounds. Wait a couple of minutes, then pour your girlfriends the first cups—they'll get fewer grounds. Lean back against a tree and think how manly you are. Accept compliments.

Planning

How Much Food per Day?

Q. How do I know how much food to pack? Should I bring a certain amount of staples like flour and biscuit mix, or should I plan separately for each meal? How much spaghetti do I need for a meal of pasta and sauce? How many dinners does a box of mac-and-cheese make?

A. The general rule for food is 2 pounds of mostly dried and/or packaged backpacking-suitable food per person per day. Figure 2½ pounds for high-mileage hikers in especially cold weather or challenging conditions. You can also calculate your food in terms of calories. Studies have shown that long-distance hikers use between 4000 and 6000 calories per day. Weekend hikers do less mileage and need fewer calories.

I know that some hikers bring actual ingredients, then turn out impressive breads and pizzas. If you have a lot of time, this is certainly a delicious option, but it requires careful planning to avoid running out of a crucial ingredient before the end of your trip.

It is much easier to use packaged meals or meals for which you can assemble the components at home. Trial and error will teach you how much food you need. As a starting point, here are some hiker-sized quantities of popular backpacking foods:

- ▲ **Freeze-dried meals.** Figure 2 to 2½ cups of cooked food per person for dinner. That works out to one standard-sized package.
- ▲ **Pasta.** A quarter pound of dried pasta makes one dinner for one person. Add packaged sauce mixes, cheese, meats, or vegetables.
- ▲ **Mac-and-cheese.** One box can make one meal if you're really hungry. Or, you can add extras like a can of meat, more cheese, some freeze-dried vegetables, and share with a partner.
- ▲ **Noodles-and-sauce mixes.** One package is one hiker dinner.
- ▲ **Soups.** You can't pack too much. A hiker can easily wolf down a whole Ramen noodle soup just for an appetizer.

Breakfast Suggestions

1. Two packages of instant oatmeal per person (add powdered milk, raisins, cinnamon)
2. A 3- or 4-ounce portion of packaged cereal per person (add powdered milk)
3. Freeze-dried eggs with bagels
4. Two pop-tarts per person
5. Selection of three nutrition or cereal bars per person (good for when you're trying to break camp quickly)
6. Ramen noodle soup

Lunch Suggestions

At least 3 ounces of cheese or peanut butter per person per lunch; or 3 ounces of salami or other dried meat per lunch. For shorter trips, canned mackerel or salmon is a nice change if you seal the can in a zipper-lock bag for packing out.
  Dried hummus
  Black bean dip
  Box of crackers
  Pita bread
  Dried fruits and nuts
  Carrot sticks

Dinner Suggestions

Start all dinners with packaged or dehydrated soup.

1. For one person: 4 ounces of uncooked pasta, one package of pesto sauce (or, for two people: 8 ounces of uncooked pasta, one 6-ounce can of tomato paste, one package of tomato sauce seasoning mix)
2. Commercially prepared freeze-dried meals
3. For two people: One package of macaroni-and-cheese with a small can of tuna, 1 ounce Parmesan cheese, one packet of freeze-dried vegetables
4. For two people: One package of stuffing mix, one package dried gravy, small amount of canned freeze-dried chicken or turkey, one package freeze-dried vegetables
5. For one person: One package of a commercial noodles-and-sauce mix (add meat, vegetables, or Parmesan cheese, if desired)
6. For one person: Four ounces couscous with homemade dehydrated sauce

▲ **Lunch.** Three ounces of cheese or peanut butter per person per lunch, plus crackers.

▲ **Breakfast.** Two packages of instant oatmeal per person per breakfast.

▲ **Snacks.** Four or five snacks spread out through the day, including cereal bars, power bars, handfuls of GORP or dried fruit, fruit bars, and the like.

Out of Food!

Q. When I start a week-long hike, my food bag seems to weigh a ton, but by the end of the week I'm scrounging for crumbs. How can I avoid running out of food?

A. Before the hike, you could use a menu planning form, which can be as simple as listing all the meals you need and checking them off as you plan them. (Some advanced hiking books, like Dan Bruce's *The Thru-Hiker's Planning Guide*, contain forms, but many hikers find this level of detailed planning to be overkill.)

On the trail, your best strategy is to start rationing from the start. First, package as much of each meal's ingredients together as practical—break up a package of pasta into three or four one-person portions and pack each portion in a plastic bag along with the sauce mix you'll need for that dinner. Once you have the meals packaged, divide them by days. Put 2 or 3 days' worth of food into one stuff sack, and 2 or 3 days' worth of food in another sack. Same goes for snacks: count them and divide them. Now you know exactly how much you have—and how much you can let yourself eat at each meal. Don't even look at the food sack that contains meals for the third and fourth days until you are on the third day of hiking. A little discipline prevents a lot of hunger!

Spices & Staples

Parmesan cheese
Dried milk
Tabasco sauce
Dried mushrooms
Dried onion flakes
Butter buds or packaged
  clarified butter
Salt and pepper
Oregano
Raisins
Cinnamon
Mustard packets
Bouillon cubes

How Much Can I Carry?

Q. How many days' worth of food can someone in pretty decent shape carry without having to resupply?

A. This is one of those questions that comes packed with its own variables: How fit are you? How heavy is your basic pack weight? What is your intended mileage? How much weight are you willing and able to haul?

Most long-distance hikers prefer to resupply about every 5 days (figure 10

A long-distance hiker opens a food drop containing pre-measured portions of everything from coffee to mac and cheese.

pounds of food). You start hearing hikers complain about heavy packs if they have to haul 7 days' (14 pounds) worth of food or more. At about the 10-day (20 pounds) point, almost everybody is seriously searching for a way to break up the load.

I consider myself an average person in terms of fitness, and while I prefer not to carry much more than 5 days' worth of food, I have managed on two or three occasions to carry as much as 17 days' worth of food. That made my pack weight a brutal 55 pounds. The flip side of the coin is that the pack only weighed 55 pounds until I ate the first candy bar—then it slowly started to lose weight. As did I!

Feeding the Hungry Hordes.

Q. I am taking a small group of teenagers backpacking, and I'm wondering what to feed them. When I asked them, they all said "pizza." That's not an option, but I would like to feed them something other than cup o' noodles.

A. Asking kids what they'd like to eat is the right idea, but as you found out, the answer might indeed be pizza, which is not exactly practical. It is, however, possible (if you are ambitious). For a backcountry recipe for this trail-food fantasy, check out *Backcountry Cooking* by Dorcas Miller (The

Mountaineers Books, 1997). Warning: Backcountry pizza requires a portable baking device such as a Bakepacker or a Dutch oven, plenty of fuel, time, and tons of patience.

Another strategy is to put the kids in charge ("Well, okay, Tommy, but *how* would you make the pizza?"). I know leaders who let kids loose in a grocery store to shop for themselves. They might end up with heavy cans, or dubious combinations, but having had input, the kids are less likely to complain. This strategy works best for an overnight trip. Anyone can put up with an "interesting" (even inedible) meal for one night. On a longer trip, you need food to be edible, not "interesting."

For a 3-night trip, you could split the group into three teams (one for each night). Have each team plan and shop for a meal for the whole group. You'd supervise the process to ensure that the quantities are about right.

One thing you'll have to decide: Are you going to do big group meals, or individual meals? Big group meals are fun, and in the long run easier to manage, but you'll need pots that can do the job. Some ideas for easy-to-make meals that most kids will enjoy:

- **Spaghetti and sauce.** Make the sauce from tomato paste and sauce seasonings, and add Parmesan cheese. Optional additions: dried mushrooms, onion flakes, oregano, and pepperoni.
- **Mac-and-cheese.** Don't just follow the directions on the package; add stuff. Choices include hunks of "real" cheese, some Parmesan, some freeze-dried vegetables, and small cans of tuna or ham.
- **Soup.** Always a good idea, soup fills the holes in a hungry hiker's stomach and helps replace lost electrolytes. There are tons of interesting instant soups in health-food stores—you don't have to settle for just plain noodles!

Finally, why not have freeze-dried meals on hand for one night? The kids can each pick their own meal. In bad weather, you'll appreciate having a no-fuss meal that requires minimal preparation. (Boil water. Stir. Eat.) Plus, the kids will probably enjoy tasting each other's food.

For more about leading groups and backpacking with kids, see Chapter 8.

Food for Discriminating Palates.

Q. I'm sorry, but those packaged noodles and freeze-dried meals look like poison to me. I know everything is supposed to taste better in the backcountry, but I've tried it—and I don't like it. Is it possible to eat really well on a hiking trip?

A. One way to eat well on the trail is to use meals you've cooked and dehydrated at home. You can dehydrate almost anything you can cook. Soups, stews, and sauces are especially good choices; you can also dry fruits, vegetables, and meats. For dinners, thick sauces and stews seem to work best. They can be served over pasta or couscous. When dehydrating at home, make sure you pack extra-large portions. What looks like a large portion at home seems smaller on the trail because foods lose some of their bulk during the drying process.

There are several guides to dehydrating available at outdoor bookstores. A popular one is *Dry It, You'll Like It!* by Gen MacManiman.

You can also check out backcountry cookbooks to learn how to make fresh meals on the trail. My preference is for cookbooks that emphasize quick and simple meals. Anything that requires an hour of chopping and simmering is probably too complicated for the backcountry—especially on a rainy night—not to mention using more fuel.

Finally, take a trip to a health-food store and an Asian food store. Both have a cornucopia of interesting foods that cook quickly and don't require refrigeration.

Cheap Eats.

Q. I'm planning a long-distance hike, and I know nutrition is important. But I'm also on a tight budget. Can you recommend some cheap, nourishing, trailworthy meals?

A. If you don't have the time or inclination to dehydrate your own food, you'll probably turn to convenient standards like pasta and cheese. Other

Trailworthy foods can be purchased at your local supermarket. This stash is being sorted for an Appalachian Trail thru-hike.

inexpensive staples are the noodles-and-sauce mixes made by companies like Lipton. A package that makes four side dishes turns out to be the perfect dinner portion for one hungry hiker. Some hikers use instant rice, instant potatoes, or stuffing mix as a base for a meal (see boxes for suggestions). Another cheap, popular backcountry staple is Ramen noodle soup.

For more nutritious (but also more expensive) foods, try some of the quick-cooking dehydrated foods available from a health-food store, like hummus and tabouli. Nutritionists also recommend using whole-grain pasta products instead of processed grains like common white pasta. Thinner pastas like angel hair cook more quickly than thicker ones like linguine. Buying from a food co-op will help keep your prices down, too.

No matter what approach you take, aim for variety. Your body works hard when hiking. Variety helps ensure a more balanced diet.

No Stove.

Q. I'm curious about hiking *sans* stove. How does the weight of stove, pots, pot-grabber, fuel, and cookable foods compare to the weight (and bulk) of foods that don't have to be cooked?

A. It's tempting, isn't it, to try to cut out those extra pounds? I sometimes go stoveless on short hikes, especially if I expect fair weather.

Here are some things to think about:

Cold food (like cheese, meat, nuts, granola, crackers) is heavier than food you have to cook. But the combined weight of fuel, pots, and a stove can weigh 3 or 4 pounds. So you need to figure out where the "break-even" point is.

For 1 or 2 days, it can make sense to go without a stove. More than that, and your pack will be lighter in the long run if you take the cooking gear, especially if you're hiking with a partner, and can share the weight.

I didn't carry a stove on recent hikes in Scotland and France, where for the most part I ate in towns and villages. When there weren't any towns, I carried cheese, canned tuna, crackers, bread, fruit, and candy bars. On the rare occasions that I had to carry food for 2 days and 2 nights, the food bags started to get heavy. But for the vast majority of the time, I didn't need a stove—and I appreciated not having to carry the extra weight of gear I rarely used. If you go the no-cook route, be aware that no-cook foods are bulkier: you have to have enough room in your pack.

A major disadvantage to no-cook hiking is that once in a while you might really want a warm meal or at least a hot drink. You could also get tired of the same foods day after day. There are two ways to cook with minimal amounts of gear.

First, if it's permissible, you could cook over a fire. Please make sure that

Hiking without a stove can mean taking advantage of delicious local cheese and bread—which weigh more but taste better.

campfires don't violate Leave-No-Trace guidelines (i.e., no fires in alpine areas, deserts, or overused sites; see Chapter 8). Use a titanium pot for both cooking and eating.

Second, make your own stove. Homemade stoves made out of (I'm not kidding about this) cat food cans and soda cans are big hits on long-distance trails. There are tons of different designs, but they all weigh in at about 2 ounces. Most run on easy-to-find denatured alcohol, although some people have designed stoves that also burn Esbitt solid fuel tabs (available in outfitting stores). (Homemade stoves take an hour or two to make. There are myriad different designs. You can check them out on the Internet under "homemade alcohol stoves.")

You'll probably have to tinker with your stove a bit to get it right (mine takes about 8 minutes to boil a liter of water at sea level; other hikers I know claim that their stoves work faster). Regardless, a few ounces of fuel, a homemade stove, and a titanium pot weigh about half a pound and give you the option of making a hot meal once in a while.

Perishability and Shelf Life

Shelf Life of Freeze-Dried Foods.

Q. I bought a ton of freeze-dried food for a thru-hike I didn't complete. Now it's sitting in my attic. How long is it good for?

A. First thing first: Get it out of your attic! The shelf life of packaged foods is affected by oxygen, moisture, and heat. The best way to prolong shelf life is to put the packages in a plastic or metal container with a tightly sealed cap, then store it in a cool place, basements being preferable to attics.

Different manufacturers claim different shelf lives for their freeze-dried foods. Some companies offer specially packaged foods with shelf lives of as much as 15 years. Shelf life depends on the specific product (vegetables last longer than seafood, for instance), the maker, and how the product is stored. Chances are that the freeze-dried food you didn't use this year will be fine next summer—and probably the summer after that, too. If the food will be hanging around for more than a couple of years, check with the manufacturer.

Foods That Don't Need Refrigeration.

Q. Can you give me a list of lunch items that are safe to eat without refrigeration? I bring fruit, but that isn't enough. I am sick of peanut butter and jelly.

A. Actually, you have a lot of choices. Most food easily lasts for several hours without needing to be refrigerated, although I'd hold the mayo. If you are concerned about hiking in really hot weather, you can buy insulated food carriers at a sporting goods store.

Cheese is a good hiking food favorite because it has plenty of calories and it can safely be carried for days (see below). One possible combination: apples, whole-grain bread, and some kind of firm-bodied cheese. Dried meats like salami, pepperoni, beef jerky, and summer sausage can all handle a few days in a pack. Boiled eggs are also fine (for day hiking, that is). If you're into health food, try pita bread with dips of hummus or black beans (both of which come in just-add-water packages). Vegetable sandwiches work well, too, for day hikes; for example, a sandwich of roasted red peppers, roasted onions, cheese, and lettuce would be a filling, tasty lunch. Pack the components separately so the bread doesn't get soggy. Choose a sturdy, whole-grain bread, both for nutritional reasons and for packability (it doesn't squash as much), and carry the vegetables in a sealed plastic container. You could also bring along some salad, although I'd stay away from wilt-prone lettuce in favor of hardier cabbage and carrots.

Cheese and Refrigeration.

Q. Cheese has to be refrigerated in stores; how long can you carry it in the backcountry without refrigeration?

A. While cheese is indeed routinely refrigerated in American homes and supermarkets, it can usually last without refrigeration for the duration of a backpacking trip. The exact number of days depends on the type of cheese and the temperature. Very oily cheeses (sharp cheddar) and very soft cheeses (Brie) don't last as long as hard aged cheeses (provolone). In between are medium-hard cheeses such as Swiss, Gouda, and Jarlsberg. I've actually carried cheese for two weeks in the summer with no problem except for some unpleasant oily residue. If cheese does start to get moldy (usually from the outside in), you can simply pare away the moldy areas.

On the Trail

Hunter-Gatherers on the Trail?

Q. I seems to me that I should be able to supplement my food by hunting, fishing, and using foods I find like mushrooms and berries. But aside from a few fishermen, I rarely see people doing this. Why not?

A. Hunting and gathering was a way of life that survived (and still survives in isolated pockets of the globe) for millions of years. But it required knowledge, skill, and energy.

The problem is that when hunters are hunting, they are in active pursuit of their quarry. When hikers are hiking, they are in active pursuit of their destination. The two don't necessarily overlap. Same goes for fishing: unless you happen to be at a lake or stream at the time of day fish are biting, you could go away hungry. Even if you do have the patience to sit around and wait, there's no guarantee that you'll catch anything.

Wild foods that you pick—like roots and shoots, berries, mushrooms, and, along the seashore, shellfish such as mussels—can add spice and flavor to your meals if you are lucky enough to find them, if you know how to identify them, and if you take the time to stop and gather them. In some places, you will certainly find enough berries to make a pancake sauce, or enough ramps (Southern wild onions) to flavor a pasta sauce. But such finds are usually the topping, not the meal.

A warning: Before you eat any wild foods, be sure you can absolutely identify them. A wild foods identification book or a laminated card with drawings of what you're looking for can be helpful. With fish and shellfish, check locally to learn about regulations, permits, and environmental hazards.

Edible Berries.

Q. How do you know what berries are safe to eat?

A. There aren't really any reliable rules of thumb that will let you safely munch your way down a berry-lined trail. True, more black and blue berries are edible than red berries; more red berries are edible than white berries. But not all dark-colored berries are edible, and not all light-colored berries are poisonous or inedible. You need to know what you're putting in your mouth.

Really, the best way to learn about any kind of edible plants—whether berries, flowers, or mushrooms—is to memorize one species at a time. Concentrate on your home area, or the area where you plan to hike. Get a good four-color guide to plants or edible foods. Study up on what one species looks like: leaves, thorns, color of ripe and unripe berries. Learn if there are any poisonous or inedible look-alikes. Then go on to the next species.

Don't make the erroneous assumption that just because a bird eats a berry, you can too. By this logic, you'd soon be munching down those little white berries produced by the poison ivy vine!

Picking huckleberries on Washington's Pacific Crest Trail

A good place to start is by learning to identify the wild relatives of berries you already know: raspberries, blackberries, strawberries, and blueberries (and their close relations, huckleberries). These are easy to recognize. If you find yourself developing more of an interest in wild foods, take a class. You'll often find them offered at a local nature center.

Pack It Out.

Q. How do I deal with all the trash that comes with packaged foods? And what about food leftovers?

A. "Pack it in, pack it out" is the slogan of the contemporary wilderness. You'll know why the first time you see a fire pit at a shelter where a careless group has left its trash behind. Nothing marks a backcountry boor more definitively than the absence of a garbage bag.

Most of your garbage (see below) will be food related. You can minimize it by carefully repackaging food in zipper-lock bags. (I wrap a rubber band around the bag; in case the zipper-lock breaks open, the rubber band holds it all together.) Get rid of all unnecessary packaging; the rest you'll have to burn or pack out. Burn only paper and cardboard, please. Aluminum foil does not burn, and your fellow campers won't appreciate the fumes from plastic garbage you throw in the communal fire. You have to pack out any food leftovers, too. Fortunately, that's rarely a problem with hikers. Plan carefully, and if you do overestimate the portions, give the rest away to fellow hikers, but not to the wildlife, no matter how hungrily they eye your mac-and-cheese supreme.

Kitchen Cleanup.

Q. What's the best way to wash dirty dishes and cooking gear, and how do you keep animals away from food remains?

A. Although many state parks provide spigots and drains for washing up, many don't. In the backcountry you'll be on your own.

Don't wash pots, pans, or dishes directly in a water source like a stream or a spring. If you're car-camping, bring along a plastic washbasin and some old plastic gallon jugs for carrying water. In the backcountry you can use a large pot as a dishpan. Use as little soap as possible—you can scour a pot with sand to remove baked-on gunk, although I usually pack a scouring pad. Then scatter the used rinsewater on the ground.

Anything that smells of food—including pots, pans, garbage, and dishes—should be securely stored out of reach of wildlife. Animals know that campgrounds are prime sources of free food, and critters from Stellar jays to black

Repackage trail foods in zipper-lock bags to minimize bulk, weight, and trash. When empty, the bags can be used for trash. Don't forget to pack them out.

bears to skunks are often found sniffing around. In bear country, special storage containers may be provided (see "Bear Canisters," Chapter 10). Most of the time, you can safely store food and cooking equipment in a locked car, but in places with bear problems be sure to follow the rules to the letter, because bears have been known to actually rip their way into locked cars—no joke! In the backcountry you should hang food and garbage bags from a tree limb securely out of reach of any bruin that happens by (see "Bear Bags," Chapter 10).

Chapter 4

Outfitting
GEAR THAT'S WORTH ITS WEIGHT

Hikers are always asking for recommendations: What kinds of boots should they buy? What pack, tent, sleeping bag, stove?

My mother taught me that it's rude to answer a question with a question. Sorry, Mom, but getting the right gear is a process of asking the right questions. What do you need the gear for? What feels right? Where will you be hiking? What fits? What do you *really* need?

Today's hikers have learned that more is not necessarily better, and that a light pack is more comfortable. But to hike with a light pack, you have to be sure that you're carrying the right stuff inside.

An entire book could be written about the subject of gear. Whole issues of magazines are devoted to the (literally) thousands of kinds of backpacks, sleeping bags, tents, stoves, mattress pads, raingear, cooksets, tarps, groundcloths, boots, and electronic gizmos that have been designed and produced so that we can live "simply" and "naturally" in the wilderness.

It would be impossible to answer every question that could be asked about every piece of gear, and by the time I did, the information about specific makes and models would be out of date. What I can do, however, is answer the questions that are most often asked about how to wade through and evaluate the cornucopia of equipment that can confuse even the most experienced outdoorsperson.

This chapter starts with an overview, then moves on to answer questions about packs, boots, tents, and other equipment. Think about what you need for the conditions where you'll be hiking. After you've decided what type of gear you want, you can find the latest makes and models in the most recent issue of *Backpacker* magazine's annual *Gear Guide*.

Gear Overview

Summer Gear List.

Q. What gear should you take on a summer hike?

A. It depends on where you're going. A Tennessee forest? A Colorado ridge? For most summer destinations, my rule is to travel light. I always take raingear, because I've gotten caught one too many times without it. But in a temperate forest, a light jacket or poncho should be enough—you don't need rain or wind pants. In high mountains, you should always tuck in an extra layer (and the rain pants, too) and the *Ten Essentials* (see box in Chapter 9).

Here's my list for summer hiking:

▲ Tent or tarp (with mosquito netting, if necessary)
▲ Lightweight sleeping bag (if in doubt, bring extra layers of clothing, not a warmer bag)
▲ Sleeping pad and groundcloth
▲ Stove, pot, pot grabber, and spoon
▲ Rain jacket
▲ Change of clothes
▲ Extra warm clothes and rain pants (if going about tree line)
▲ Food
▲ Personal items, including knife, bug dope, sunscreen, sunglasses
▲ Sun hat
▲ Water filter, water bottle, and water bag
▲ Boots and clothes to hike in

Technical Shmechnical.

Q. I'm trying to find a definition for the word "technical" as it's used in hiking magazines and outdoor stores. I see references to technical packs, technical clothing, technical this, and technical that. But no one can tell me what it actually means when applied to hiking gear. Can you help?

A. Sure, technical means brighter colors and a higher price tag. Okay, I admit that I'm being facetious. But seriously, I know what you mean about those ads promising "high-tech," "technical," "performance," "ultimate," and "extreme" gear. Advertisers know that buyers of high-priced outerwear are more likely to wear it to the mall than to Mount Everest. They know that the only ice climbing most people do is to stumble over the pile the snowplow shoved up against their cars. They also know that consumers gravitate to stuff that promises it can survive the world's toughest tests on the world's highest mountains.

I'm not aware of any rulebook that says when the adjective technical should and shouldn't be used. Generally, it refers to gear that is designed to be used in extreme conditions or in situations that demand technical skills. I'd define these as being skills you can't learn from a book—they are skills someone has to teach you, skills you have to practice to master.

Gear that earns its "technical" label is carefully engineered. For example, a "technical" pack should have a well-designed suspension system and high-quality components, along with doodads that let you attach other gear like ice tools or an ax. Technical outerwear should be both breathable and waterproof, with features that let you make adjustments if you are too hot or too cold.

The bottom line, of course, is that you need the right gear for the conditions you'll be facing—and that means not wasting your money on gear that out-performs your recreation. My three-season tent, for example, is anything but technical. You simply don't need to spend $600 on a mountaineering tent to hike the Appalachian Trail in June. And there's no reason to pay for and carry a pack with a crampon guard if you never use crampons.

But you can bet that my winter climbing jacket and pants are "technical." I even have a "technical" hat for the desert. (I'll admit I was a little leery of buying it—I mean, really, a technical *hat?!* But in fact, it was intelligently designed to solve real desert problems, and it turned out to be one of the best pieces of gear I own.)

So rely on your own needs and judgment. And remember—in the end, the manufacturers decide what they call technical. You decide what you need. Caveat Emptor.

Sticker Shock.

Q. I'm just starting to collect backpacking gear, and I'm on a budget. Mostly I plan to hike in the summer. Is it really necessary to spend a fortune to spend a night in the woods? Why does this stuff cost so much, and how can I shave some money off my gear budget?

A. I know that gear seems expensive, especially if you're buying it all at once. If it's any consolation, you can always consider that once you've bought the stuff it will (a) last for years and (b) enable you to take cheap vacations virtually anywhere in the world.

If you can't afford to buy everything you'd like all at once, don't despair!

To start out you can rent gear (which gives you the chance to try before you buy) or share some equipment with a friend. You can make some inexpensive substitutions, which will allow you to start backpacking with minimal expense. (Please note: Some of these substitutions are appropriate for temperate summer weather. In high mountains, you may need more or tougher gear.)

▲ Instead of a tent, use a tarp.
▲ Instead of a rain jacket and rain pants, use a poncho.
▲ Instead of hiking boots, wear running shoes.
▲ Instead of buying special pots and utensils, rummage through your kitchen cabinet for pots and old plastic bowls.
▲ Instead of expensive proprietary technical clothing, use cheaper polypropylene.
▲ Instead of buying a water bottle, use an empty soda bottle.
▲ Instead of buying a warmer sleeping bag, use your old bag and sleep in extra layers of clothing.
▲ Buy used gear or factory seconds.

Useful Stuff.

Q. I am planning a trip with some friends and I wanted to know what you suggest we take beyond the basics. I want to know more about things new hikers might not know about taking that seasoned hikers would.

A. The answer to this question is the opposite of what you might think. Seasoned hikers don't take more stuff, they take less. You can tell the hiker with the most mileage on his or her boots by the amount of stuff that's *not* in the pack.

Nonetheless, you're right: some hikers get attached to equipment that not everyone would think to carry. Here's a list of some of the "little" items I've found helpful. (Note: Not everyone carries them, and I don't carry each item on every trip.)

▲ **A bandanna.** It can be used as a washcloth, to mop up the wet floor of a tent on a rainy day, as a napkin, as a pre-filter for gunky water, as a sweatband, and in a dozen other ways.
▲ **Duct tape.** This traditional backcountry fix-all can be used to patch an air mattress, hold together a torn sleeping bag, keep delaminating soles from falling off your boots, and as first aid for blisters.
▲ **Walking sticks.** If you have knee problems (see Chapter 9), these can change your hike from a limp to a lark.
▲ **Cord.** Use it as clothesline, to tie stuff to your pack, or to hang food out of reach of animals.
▲ **Space blanket.** This serves as a perfect groundcloth, plus it can be used as

an emergency shelter or raingear.

▲ **Garbage bags.** Use them as emergency raingear, a pack cover, for sitting on wet ground, for waterproofing stuff sacks, and of course, for packing out garbage.

▲ **Bungee cords.** Need to carry snowshoes? Dry some laundry on the back of your pack? Attach an air mattress or tent poles to the pack? Bungees to the rescue!

▲ **Whistle.** Its sound carries farther than a voice. Whistles are especially useful when hiking off-trail in foggy weather.

▲ **Baking soda.** Uses include deodorant (don't forget your feet), toothpaste, and water-bottle freshener.

▲ **Closed-cell foam pad.** In winter, an additional sleeping pad provides warmth and comfort at night. In the daytime, sit on it during breaks to reduce the amount of heat your body loses to the cold ground.

▲ **Pouch.** Worn on your hipbelt, a pouch can keep necessaries like insect repellent and sunscreen close at hand.

▲ **Hydration system.** You'll drink more if you don't have to take off your pack every time you're thirsty. Your "system" might simply be a pouch that holds your water bottle in a place you can easily reach, or a bladder with tubes to sip through as you're walking.

▲ **Repair kit.** Need I say more?

Weighing In.

Q. Whenever I read gear reviews or look at catalogs, I see different weights for the same piece of gear. And sometimes neither of those weights is accurate. How do I really know how much a piece of gear weighs?

A. If I'm in doubt, I ask to weigh the item on the store's scale. (If a store ships merchandise, it has a scale somewhere in the back.) I've found huge variations (sometimes as much as 25 percent) between the advertised weight and the actual weight. The problem became so ubiquitous that a few years ago *Backpacker* magazine started printing both the advertised weight and the actual tested weight of the product.

There are a couple of reasons for discrepancies. Manufacturers often include extra items, like a whole tube of seam-seal compound or extra tent stakes, in the package. They say that since you're probably not going to take all those items along, the weight of the extra stuff they throw in shouldn't count. Each manufacturer used to count whatever it wanted as the weight of the item. Most manufacturers now advertise a "packaged" weight, which includes the weight of everything that is sold in the package, and a "field" weight, which includes only the most basic components needed to use the item. Since "field weight" sometimes doesn't include such essentials as tent stakes, the true weight of what you'll actually carry is somewhere in between.

There's another issue: so-called variables in manufacturing, which can lead to differences among individual products. Such variations should not, however, be more than a few ounces.

Since we'll probably never have a fool-proof system, due diligence is up to you. Double-check the weight yourself.

What Does Ultralight Mean?

Q. I've been seeing words like "ultralight" and "lightweight" used to advertise gear. Is there a difference? What should I be looking for?

A. There are dictionaries of music and geography and finance and bibles and law, but to my knowledge, no one has yet published a dictionary of terms for outdoor equipment. We're left to our own devices.

Certainly, it can be frustrating to see a two-person tent advertised as "lightweight"—only to learn that it weighs upward of 7 pounds! To choose the right gear, you have to go beyond the hype.

Over the last few years, hikers have started to agree about some common-sense definitions.

A "traditional" backpacker goes out with the kind of load you've seen a million times on trails and in magazine photos. Much of the well-made, time-tested, mid-range equipment on the market falls into the "traditional" category.

"Lightweight" gear shaves ounces and sometimes pounds off of traditional gear without sacrificing much in the way of function. Weight savings are achieved either by cutting back on extra features, or by using superior materials. Examples of a bare-bones lightweight design might include a 4-pound two-person tent. (It may not be as roomy, and it may not be free-standing, but it's still a tent.) Another example would be a 3-or 4-pound backpack—it might not have the same comfy hipbelt or solid frame, but it still *has* a hipbelt and a frame. Examples of the high-tech approach would include 20-degree sleeping bags that weigh less than 2 pounds because of superior down. A titanium pot is another example of using high-tech materials to reduce weight.

Are You a Lightweight?

You can tell if you're a traditional, lightweight, or ultralight hiker by applying the following "test" to your gear. In summer, not counting food and water, how much does your fully loaded pack weigh?

20–25 pounds: You're as traditional as mom and apple pie.

15–20 pounds: You're a lightweight, and looking quite svelte.

Under 15 pounds: You're a true ultralight hiker. Just be sure you have what you need to stay safe out there.

"Ultralight" gear is entirely a different idea. Ultralight hikers challenge everything about hiking. They don't merely try to find the lightest tent; they question whether they even need a tent, and come up with alternate shelters like tarps or tarp-tents. Often, they make sacrifices in both function and comfort. They might make equipment do double duty: in some ultralight backpacks, for example, a closed-cell-foam mattress is folded and placed in the pack in such a way that it acts as a frame. Or they go without—for example, by not using hipbelts.

Note that many true "ultralight" manufacturers started as small mom-and-pop operations. Recently some of the more successful small firms have been purchased by established companies, leading to some overlap (and confusion) between the categories.

Ultralight Hiking: Safe or Stupid?

Q. I'm attracted to the comfort of ultralight hiking, but I worry about what would happen in inclement weather. What is your opinion of the safety of ultralight hiking methods?

A. I'm not a fan of any single method of hiking, ultralight or otherwise. There are many effective ways to hike. For the most part, strict ultralight methods don't work for me, although that doesn't mean that they won't work for you. And yes, some of my concerns are safety-related. Here are a few issues to think about as you try to pare down your load.

Safety. A low-weight, high-mileage style of hiking requires that you strip down the weight of what you're carrying to the bare minimum—in which case, you might not have what you need in an emergency. If you don't have the gear you need, you have to be fit enough to walk however far it takes to get out of trouble. I've been in a few hairy situations—they happen fast and hard—and I've seen way too many people carted out of the mountains by search-and-rescue teams. So I prefer to err on the side of that extra fleece jacket and rain pants.

Distance. Do you really want to do the big miles? The ultralight hiking movement is most popular among long-distance hikers who cover huge distances: sometimes 30 or 40 miles a day. I've run a couple of marathons and done a triathlon, so although my fitness has varied considerably over the years, I do have some experience of what it's like to be ultra-fit. But even when I was most fit, I really didn't like hiking 30 miles a day. It didn't matter how light my pack was. Benton MacKaye once said that the purpose of hiking was "to walk, to see, and to see what you see." I'm not sure how much you can see when you're racing along a trail. Given that I'm not interested in mega-mileage, I don't mind carrying a little extra in the interest of safety.

The Pacific Crest Trail in southern California is a good place to consider the pros and cons of going ultralight.

Foot injuries. Wearing sneakers is a popular ultralight trend, but not everyone can hike successfully in sneakers. I first hiked in sneakers in 1988, and have since hiked more than a thousand miles in them. But on the Pacific Crest Trail (PCT), using sneakers led to severe inflammation of heel spurs I didn't know I had. It was so painful I thought my hike was over. Stress fractures are another potential problem. One year, I saw several sneaker-wearing hikers hobbling around Tuolumne Meadows in casts, getting ready to leave the PCT! At least one of them had seemed to be a perfect candidate for ultralight, ultra-distance hiking—his pack's base weight was 15 pounds, and at the start of the trail he was in good shape, covering 20–25 miles a day. But he overdid it.

Back and shoulder injuries. The same goes for ultralight packs: Some of us need traditional designs with load lifters and padded belts. A couple of summers ago, I carried a very light, seemingly comfortable internal-frame pack with a maximum weight of only 15–18 pounds (including food and water). But I later developed a severe rotator cuff injury. Such injuries are uncommon among backpackers with traditional loads, but are seen more frequently among people who make their own packs or use packs with minimal load-supporting mechanisms. Much more important than how much a pack weighs is how it feels. It's no fun to hike in pain. Remember, no matter how light your pack, food still weighs 2 pounds for every day, and water weighs about 2 pounds a liter. Say you're hiking in a desert where you have to carry 4 days' worth of food and about 6 liters of water. That's 20 pounds in addition to the base weight of your equipment. The total may be too heavy for an ultralight pack to comfortably handle.

All that said, many people have successfully used lightweight methods. By all means, experiment. Try out new techniques gradually, taking into consideration *your* style, *your* fitness, *your* goals, *your* comfort level, and *your* capacity to get yourself out of trouble if you find yourself in it.

And remember the long-distance hiking motto: Hike Your Own Hike.

Does Your Backpack Need to Go on a Diet?

Q. While I think I am packing lightly, my pack always seem to weigh a lot. On a recent weeklong summer trip, it weighed about 50 pounds. It would have been heavier, but I split communal gear with a partner. My sleeping bag weighs 6 pounds, and my sleeping pad weighs 5 pounds. I carry a stove, a water filter, a small pot for boiling water, a first-aid kit, enough food for the week, and clothes. We split the tent poles, tarp (groundcloth), stakes, and tent (9 pounds). I would love to get rid of weight but have no idea how to do it. I can think of a few things that I could leave behind, but nothing significant. Any ideas?

A. Join the club. The club, that is, of backpackers always scheming to reduce their pack weight.

A lot of people start out with unnecessary stuff, but that doesn't seem to be your problem. Your problem is the weight of your core gear. It sounds like some of your equipment is better suited for car-camping than backpacking. Let's take a look at the major items and talk about how much they *should* weigh.

First off, the tent: No way should you be lugging around 9 pounds for shelter in summer! Figure 6 pounds max for a two-person, three-season tent. Some lightweight tents fit two (friendly) adults at as little as 4 pounds. The two-person tent I use is spacious enough for two adults to sit up in, and weighs about 5¼ pounds. Even better (in non-buggy conditions), have you considered a tarp? An 8-by-9-foot tarp is more than adequate for two adults and weighs less than 2 pounds, including stakes and cords.

Next up: your groundcloth. You shouldn't be using a tarp as a groundcloth. For just a few ounces, you can get a lightweight "footprint" to fit under your tent. Or use a space blanket. Or at least cut the tarp down to size.

And did you really say a 5-*pound* sleeping pad? What are you sleeping on—a Sealy Posturepedic? A full-length ultra-luxurious hiking air mattress weighs about 2 pounds. The skimpier three-quarter-length lightweight models are about 1 pound. Or you could use an even lighter closed-cell-foam pad.

As for your sleeping bag, one of my store-brand 20-degree sleeping bags weighs less than 3 pounds. Lighter, but more expensive, 20-degree bags weighing 2 pounds or less are also available.

If you pare down those items alone, you can easily drop 10 pounds.

What Should Your Gear Weigh?

ITEM	ULTRALIGHT	LIGHTWEIGHT	TRADITIONAL
Tent or tarp (for two)	less than 4 lbs	4–5½ lbs	more than 5½ lbs
Backpack	less than 3 lbs	3–5 lbs	more than 5 lbs
Raingear (jacket and pants)	less than 1 lb	1–2 lbs	more than 2 lbs
Sleeping bag (20 degrees)	less than 2 lbs	2–3 lbs	more than 3 lbs
Stove and fuel	homemade stove	wood-burning stove	white gas stove
Sleeping pad	¾ length closed-cell foam	¾ length air mattress	full-length air mattress
Boots	sneakers	leather/fabric hybrids	leather boots

Packs

Internal versus External.

Q. I need a backpack for three-season hiking. I usually do one or two weeklong trips a year, as well as a couple of long weekends in the spring and fall. Should I get an internal-frame pack or an external-frame pack?

A. Although packs are usually divided into the categories of "internal frame" and "external frame," I think that size, fit, weight, comfort, and price are all more important considerations.

However, there are some functional differences. Here are some criteria to consider.

Choose an internal-frame pack:

- If you think you'll be traveling on buses and planes with the pack. Internal-frame packs are less likely to get bent and mangled by baggage handlers.
- If you do a lot of winter hiking. An internal-frame pack better protects your gear from snow because most of your equipment goes inside one big main compartment.
- If you do a lot of off-trail hiking and scrambling. Internal-frames fit more snugly, with a lower center of gravity.

Choose an external-frame pack:

- If you're on a tight budget. External-frame packs are a little less expensive.
- If you spend most of your time on well-groomed trails that don't involve a lot of rock-scrambling.
- If you like a variety of different pouches for organizing your gear.
- If you plan on doing a lot of hot-weather or desert hiking. The external-frame pack is a little cooler because it puts some distance between your sweaty back and the pack.

Many hikers prefer internal frame packs, which hug the body.

The classic external frame pack has stood the test of time.

How Big a Pack Do I Need?

Q. I'm going on a month-long trip this summer in the Rocky Mountains. Will the pack I use for shorter trips be big enough? How large a pack will I need?

A. It's a common fallacy that a longer trip requires a bigger pack. Actually, some of the smallest packs you'll see in the backcountry belong to people who are going the longest distances. Maybe it's because the more you walk, the more you learn what you don't need.

Also, almost no one actually goes out for a month-long trip without re-supplying. If you'll be resupplying once a week, you don't need a pack that can hold all your supplies for a month; you need a pack that can hold enough supplies for a week. Be sure to pack non-edible consumables (shampoo, film, map and guidebook sections, bug repellent, sunscreen, toothpaste, and soap) in your resupply boxes, too, so you don't carry more than you need. Your total load shouldn't be any more than it would be to go on a weeklong hike.

Another reason to stay away from big packs is the more space you have, the more stuff you might be lured into carrying! Not to mention the plaintive pleas from your hiking partner to "just take the tent because you've got all that extra room."

Long-Distance Backpacks.

I'm hoping to hike one of the long trails. I am starting to choose equipment and need a backpack. I have no clue what to look for. Are there any particular considerations for long-distance hikes?

A. To choose a pack, you'll need to know how much stuff you really think you'll be carrying. I know, this is a chicken-and-egg question, because you need some experience to answer it, and to get experience, you need a pack. Here are a few pointers:

▲ In typical three-season conditions, even with a traditional load, you should be able to get your pack weight well under 40 pounds, including food and water, the pack, and everything in it. So you're looking for a medium-capacity pack—somewhere in the 4000–5000-cubic-inch capacity. Stay away from words like "monster load" and "expedition."

▲ Comfort is really the main concern, because on a longer hike, you're going to be living with that pack. I'd suggest going on a couple of long trial hikes with rental packs to see what your back feels like after 15 miles and 4000 feet of elevation gain. When you go to buy your pack, be sure it's custom fitted for you. Outdoor retailers perform this service.

▲ Long-distance hikers appreciate features like good padding around the hips, plenty of load-adjustment options, and extra pockets to keep essential items like lunch and raingear handy. A pack that can be converted to a daypack is useful for "slackpacking," peak-bagging, or doing errands. Don't get carried away with too many added features—the fewer the seams, belts, buckles, and moveable parts, the fewer things there are to break.

▲ Consider the manufacturer. *Backpacker* magazine's annual *Gear Guide* lists currents models made by major manufacturers, with editorial notes. Most outdoor magazines also run gear tests that compare various makes and models. The reason you want to go with a major manufacturer with a good reputation is that they offer good warranties and customer support if you have problems in the field.

Waterproof Packs.

Q. I'm planning a trip to New Zealand and I've heard it can be wickedly wet. How can I keep my pack dry? Don't they make waterproof backpacks?

A. For years, truly waterproof backpacks have been an ideal that (among hikers, at least) existed in the realm of imagination and desire alongside the Holy Grail and nuclear fusion. The dry-bags used by kayaking and rafting folks are effective, but too heavy for hikers. Apparently, making a dry-*pack* that we hikers can carry without turning into beasts of unbearable burden is harder than you would think.

We're beginning to see some progress. A few waterproof backpacks are now available. They are lined with a layer of polyurethane, and weigh about the same as traditional packs. The selection is still very small, and the packs do leak a little.

For most people, the best option is still the old-fashioned pack cover on the outside, and waterproof stuff sacks on the inside.

In New Zealand, by the way (where I once experienced 12 inches of rain in a 48-hour period!), Kiwi trampers line their packs with heavy waterproof plastic bags (available for sale at their Department of Conservation offices). Garbage bags work, too. Sleeping bags and clothing should be protected the most vigilantly, but with a little care all your gear should stay dry.

Pack Fitting.

Q. I keep seeing references to torso length. I'm five-foot-nine. How I do know what my torso length is?

A. Actually, torso length has nothing to do with your height. Three people can be exactly the same height and have completely different torso lengths.

To properly measure the length of your torso, you'll need to find your C-7 vertebra and your "iliac crest." Wait! Don't panic! It's not brain surgery!

The C-7 vertebra is the base of your neck where the bump is. The iliac crest is near the small of your back: to find it, turn your hands so that the thumbs face backwards, then rest your hands on your hipbones; your thumbs now point to the iliac crest. The distance between the C-7 and the iliac crest is your torso length.

How the torso length translates to actual pack size depends on the manufacturer. For example, some manufacturers only make one size (which may not fit all—be sure it fits you!). Others offer four or five different sizes. If you're an "average" size (say, between 16 and 20 inches), you're in luck. There are literally hundreds of packs that will fit you. But don't despair if you're unusually small or large, pack sizes on the market range from a small 14 inches (and sometimes even less) to 24 inches (and sometimes more).

Tents

Tent Types.

Q. Do I really need a free-standing tent?

A. Free-standing tents offer hassle-free pitching and can be moved around to test-drive the absolute single best sleeping spot (good for Princess-and-the-Pea types). They're great if you have to move because your site turns out to be tilted or the wind direction suddenly shifts. But they are not necessary in most circumstances, and they are often heavier than their non-free-standing counterparts. Note that free-standing tents usually have at least one or two stakes that must be driven in the ground to hold out the vestibule or pull out a rain fly.

Free-standing tents *do* make sense if you plan to pitch your tent on very hard ground. True, no one actually *hopes* to be sleeping on a slab of concrete. But there are some camping situations where you'll be glad you don't have to mess with stakes:

▲ Wooden tent platforms, which are often required in established campsites in fragile environments.
▲ Old roads. Even dirt roads can be so hard that is impossible to drive in a stake.
▲ Above tree line on gravelly ground. Stakes may be difficult to drive in.

Above tree line in Washington's Goat Rocks Wilderness, a free-standing tent is easier to pitch on the hard, gravelly ground.

Tents with a lot of mosquito netting let in sunlight and fresh air.

Claustrophobic in Tents.

Q. I am looking for alternatives to traditional tents, which I find heavy, claustrophobic, and isolating. Is there a non-tent shelter that offers protection from wind, rain, and bugs?

A. It's a tall order to find a shelter that can protect you from everything nature can throw your way (from hailstones to blackflies) and still let you feel like you aren't claustrophobically trapped in a nylon envelope.

Some hikers use a tarp plus mosquito netting. You'd have to experiment to figure out how and where to attach the netting to the tarp. (It'll depend on how you like to pitch a tarp; see below.) Some small companies have started making lightweight tarp tents, which can be pitched with walking sticks. They provide adequate shelter in temperate conditions, but they are not free-standing. Most of the models I've seen don't handle high winds especially well.

There are a few strategies you can use to minimize bug problems when you use tarps. First, choose a breezy campsite. That's breezy—not blustery! Be sure you pitch the tarp securely enough to withstand a steady wind.

Second, be sure your sleeping bag is not too warm. If your bag is too heavy, you'll sleep outside of it, exposing your skin to every hungry mosquito in the neighborhood. On very hot nights, use a lightweight liner to put a layer between your skin and the bugs that want to bite it.

Another point: Not all tents are heavy and isolating. Some have interior walls made mostly of mosquito netting. These can be very light; some weigh less than 4 pounds for two people. Using just the tent body in good weather lets you look out at what's going on around you. In bad weather, you simply add the rain fly.

Above tree line, tents make a lot of sense because it's hard to stake a tarp securely on rocky terrain. So when I expect to camp above tree line, I always take a free-standing tent.

Hammock Tents.

Q. I love hanging out in a hammock in my yard. I've seen hammock tents on the market. What are their advantages and disadvantages?

A. Hammock tents are gaining a small but enthusiastic chorus of supporters. If you're a hammock kind of guy (or gal) they might work for you.

You can pitch a hammock anywhere there are trees, especially if the hammock has adjustable cords. (Look for designs that have minimum-impact webbing that won't dig into the bark of the tree.) If you do a lot of forest camping, hammocks offer a much wider selection of campsites because you don't have to worry about muddy ground, stones, rocks, and roots. Above tree line, of course, hammocks are a lousy choice.

Some people find themselves too cold in hammocks because cold air can seep in from underneath you. One solution to this problem is to sleep on top of a light, insulating pad. But that doesn't work for everyone.

Another disadvantage: As comfortable as hammocks are in the backyard, after several hours your back might start to feel sore from the lack of support. Some hammocks are designed to help you "sleep straight," but you'll have to try them yourself to see if you find them comfortable.

Why a Groundcloth?

Q. I've always put the groundcloth inside my tent, but some other hikers said it's supposed to go outside the tent. Who is right?

A. They are (sorry 'bout that!). The groundcloth goes under the tent not just to keep moisture from wicking through the floor, but in order to protect the fragile and expensive tent fabric from ripping and tearing on twigs, pinecones, cactus spines, and sharp stones.

When you put the tent on top of the groundcloth, be sure to tuck in any parts of the groundcloth that might be sticking out. If it rains during the night, water can collect on the groundcloth and leak into the tent.

Waking Up Wet.

Q. When it rains at night, pools of water collect at the bottom of my tent. How can I stop this from happening?

A. There are several reasons you could be waking up doing the breaststroke.

First is your choice of a campsite. Sometimes, campsites have been used so many times that they actually form little depressions where water easily pools. Another possibility: your tent site is in the natural runoff path that water takes in a heavy rain.

The second reason your tent might be leaking is that it's poorly pitched. Did you remember to tuck in the groundcloth so it wouldn't collect water? Did you pull the guylines taut so the tent would shed water properly? Did you take advantage of natural windbreaks?

And third: Did you seam-seal your tent properly? Many tents now come factory sealed, but manufacturers often overlook tiny little seams in corners. Go over the seams yourself to ensure that your tent really is shipshape.

Picking a well-drained campsite minimizes the chance that water will pool under your tent if it rains.

In heavy winter conditions, you need a full-fledged mountaineering tent.

Using a Three-Season Tent in Four Seasons.

Q. I love my three-season tent and don't want to spend money on a new tent that I'll only use a couple of times a year. Can I use my three-season tent in the winter?

A. Maybe. It depends on what kind of tent you have and how severe the conditions are.

There are three concerns with using three-season tents in the winter:

Space. In winter, you carry a lot more stuff. If your three-season tent is skimpy in size, it might be too small for winter's extra equipment and clothing.

Snow and cold protection. Many three-season tents use netting instead of fabric for the interior walls, which provides bug protection and ventilation. However, in winter you don't have to worry about bug protection, and too much ventilation means you could get cold. Also, spindrift snow can blow in through the mosquito netting.

Strength. Winter tents have stronger poles that won't snap under a heavy load of snow. Some three-season tents can't handle snow well. The popular wedge-shaped model, for example, has a flattish top that doesn't shed snow, so you have to bang snow off the roof all night.

However, if your tent has a shape that will shed snow, if it's not *too* well ventilated, and if you're not taking it someplace where meteorologists routinely broadcast stories about blizzards of the century, then a three-season tent might work for the fourth season.

Pitching a Tarp.

Q. I keep reading that tarps are an alternative to tents, but how do you pitch them to keep wind and rain out?

A. A standard tarp is simply a square (or rectangular) piece of nylon with grommets running along the sides. The two most common ways to pitch it are a symmetrical A-frame, and a lopsided lean-to. The A-frame gives more protection; the lean-to shape gives more living space.

Tarps can be pitched using trees or hiking sticks to hold them up, and some cord and a few tent stakes to anchor them to the ground. You'll need to practice to get the hang of it. The objective is a good, taut pitch. You should be able to bounce a quarter off the nylon!

A few hints:

▲ Use telescoping hiking poles as ridgepoles. With telescoping poles, you are not dependent on finding the right tree, and you have the flexibility to pitch the tarp at any height you choose.

▲ Be sure the tarp is taut; if it isn't, it will fall down in a strong wind. Try to shake it. If it can't withstand a hearty shake, it might not withstand a storm.

▲ Take advantage of natural windbreaks such as copses of trees, bushes, and large boulders when pitching a tarp.

A tarp pitched as a lean-to

▲ If you pitch a tarp in a lean-to shape, the more open side should face away from the wind, and the closed side should face into the wind.

▲ Some large tarps are made of two pieces of material sewn together. If there is a seam, be sure it is sealed. Small tubes of seam-sealing compound are available at outfitting stores. You simply apply the compound to the seams to plug up the holes made by the needle during the sewing process.

Cleaning a Tent.

Q. What's the best way to clean a tent? Do I just throw it in the washing machine? Or do I have to have it dry-cleaned?

A. Neither! Both can damage your tent beyond repair.

Chances are all your tent needs is a good rinsing. Pitch it in your backyard and gently run water from a hose over it. Wash trouble spots with a gentle detergent soap. Then let it air out and dry completely before storing it. You can strengthen the waterproofing on your tent by applying a water-repellency treatment like Nikwax, available in most outfitting stores.

If you put your tent away wet, you're creating a perfect environment for mildew and mold. A tent that has mildew on it can sometimes be saved. One repair and cleaning service recommends cleaning mildew-stained tents with a solution of 1 gallon of hot water and a half a cup of Lysol. After the tent has dried, mix another gallon of hot water with 1 cup of salt and 1 cup of concentrated lemon juice. Apply this to the tent, and let it dry.

Sleeping Bags

Down versus Synthetic.

Q. I'm shopping for a bag for three-season hiking. Should I get a down bag or a synthetic bag?

A. It used to be that any outdoorsperson worth his GORP had a down bag. Down bags were lighter, more compressible, and warmer ounce for ounce. Synthetic substitutes were heavy and took up so much space it looked like you were hauling grandma's feather bed in your pack.

But today's synthetics give down a run for its money, sometimes offering the same temperature ratings at virtually the same weight, if not the same price (down is usually, although not always, more expensive).

Down remains the choice among many serious mountaineers, and it's a good choice for winter camping because it is more compressible (a useful feature in winter, when your pack never seems big enough to hold all your stuff). Prime-quality down still offers more warmth per ounce. But for backpackers hiking in more temperate three-season conditions, the difference is actually quite insignificant.

Down has one disadvantage: it completely loses its insulating capacity when wet. Although it takes a lot of carelessness (perhaps even effort) to soak a down sleeping bag, if you spend the bulk of your hiking time in predictably rainy climates, a synthetic bag is probably a better choice.

The major disadvantage of synthetic bags is that they are less compressible than down. If you have a small backpack, it can be a hassle to try to fit a synthetic bag inside. This can also be a problem with very warm winter bags, even those made of down. So before buying any bag, make sure it fits into your pack.

Sleeping Bag Ratings Problems.

Q. I bought a 30-degree bag, but I'm freezing in it, even when the temperature is well above 40. Why? What did I do wrong?

A. You probably didn't do anything wrong at all.

Sleeping bag ratings are inconsistent from manufacturer to manufacturer. One 20-degree bag may feel toasty, and another may feel full of drafts and cold air. A recent attempt to standardize ratings proved impractical because of the number of variables, which include the fact that people's bodies are different. The bag that keeps me warm at night may leave you shivering. Some manufacturers give you two numbers: a survival number, and a comfort number.

Look for the following features in a sleeping bag to make sure it keeps you as warm as possible:

- A good fit. Try on a sleeping bag just like you would try on clothes. Crawl into it in the store. Roll around on the floor. If it's too tight, your body will compress the fill, making it less efficient. If it's too loose (especially if it's too long) there will be too much air for your body to heat up, and you will "sleep colder."
- A snug hood. You lose heat through your head.
- Draft tubes that run up the length of the bag's zipper. These keep warm air in and drafts out.
- Loft. Compare bags by laying them out next to each other on the floor. The thicker, fluffier one will be warmer, even if the two bags have the same rating.

Four-Season Bags.

Q. I am looking for a four-season down sleeping bag. I've heard that down is cool in summer and warm in winter. Is that the way it works?

A. Unfortunately, that's not the way down works. There really isn't such a thing as a sleeping bag that will keep you comfortable in all four seasons.

Down works by trapping air. Your body heat warms the trapped air, and that's what insulates you. The bigger and fluffier the bag, the more air it traps, and the warmer you stay.

There are three reasons why some down bags are warmer than others:

- The amount of down in the bag. More down traps more air.
- The quality of the down. An ounce of high-quality goose down will trap more air than an ounce of lower-quality down. Down quality is measured in units of "fill"—the higher the number, the better. The type of down will be described on the tag.
- Design. Good-quality winter mummy bags are tight-fitting so that your body doesn't have to heat too much air. However, make sure the fit isn't too tight, because in really cold weather you'll probably be wearing a lot of extra clothes.

Sleeping bags can be comfortable in a range of temperatures, especially if you use features like the foot zippers (opening them lets warm air escape) and the hood. The range differs from person to person, but I find that if a bag is rated down to 20 degrees, it will usually be comfortable up to about 50 degrees. If it gets warmer, I'll unzip the bag and use it like a blanket. There's nothing wrong with carrying a sleeping bag that's a little too warm, except that it's heavier than it needs to be. But at some point, even if it's unzipped, a heavy winter bag will simply be too warm for summer conditions.

Maintaining Sleeping Bag Loft.

Q. My down sleeping bag used to keep me warm down to 20 degrees; now, I'm shivering even when the temperature is above freezing. And the bag looks skimpier. Is there anything I can do?

A. Your bag may simply need a good washing. Over time, oils and dirt collect and start to damage the down.

Down sleeping bags can be machine-washed or washed by hand (never dry-cleaned, which breaks down the insulation and leaves a toxic chemical residue). Most manufacturers recommend machine washing on the gentle cycle of a front-loading washer. You may have to go through the rinse cycle a couple of times to get all the soap out of the down. You'll have the same rinsing problem if you wash the bag by hand. You can dry most bags in a clothes drier set to the air-dry setting. You may have heard that you should throw in a tennis shoe to break up the clumps of down, but that can damage the down. You could use several tennis balls for the last few minutes of the cycle. Check with the manufacturer of your bag for directions, including recommended soaps and detergents. If you don't want to do the job yourself, many manufacturers and outdoor gear repair companies will do it for you.

If washing doesn't do the trick, it may be that your bag needs a down transplant. Again, either the manufacturer or a gear repair company can add a few ounces of new down to a tired bag. It will be a little heavier than it was, but it'll have more loft.

Finally, between hikes store the bag loose, out of its stuff sack. Too much compression will damage the down over time.

Lovebirds and Sleeping Bags.

Q. I'm planning a trip with my wife. Is there any way to put two sleeping bags together?

A. Most bags made by major American manufacturers use zippers with the same teeth and fasteners, so you can zip bags together, even if they are different brands. However, one has to be "left zipping" and one has to be "right zipping." Also, they should be similar sizes and shapes, or they won't match up.

You can also buy an attachment that holds your air mattresses together so they won't slide away from each other during the night.

Sleeping together sounds like it should be warmer than sleeping alone, but in the backcountry it isn't, because warm air escapes through the open areas of the joined bags near the shoulders. There is, however, a new lightweight insert called a sleeping bag doubler that, when zipped to a single sleeping bag, turns the bag into a blanket big enough for two, with draft tubes around the shoulders. So in addition to solving the draft problem, it reduces the weight because you only have to carry one bag!

Making a Bag Warmer.

Q. I have a 30-degree bag, but I'm thinking of going on a hike where the temperatures could drop below freezing. Do I need to buy another bag?

A. Probably not.

If you find that your 30-degree bag keeps you warm in 30-degree temperatures, you can extend its downward range. Here's how:

▲ Sleep in a tent. Better yet, sleep in a tent with a hiking partner. The tent holds warm air in, raising the effective air temperature. Two bodies create more hot air than one.

▲ Add a liner. Fleece and silk sleeping bag liners feel nice against your skin and keep the bag warm (and clean; the liner is much easier to wash than the bag). Fleece bags add warmth, although they can be heavy.

- Use a vapor-barrier liner. This is a sleeping bag liner made of non-breathable material. Your body heat stays close to your body (so, unfortunately, does your sweat). The advantages: You stay warmer, and less condensation collects on your tent.
- Wear more clothes. (Not fewer—although it's a common misconception, sleeping nude inside a sleeping bag does *not* make you warmer.) Layers trap air, which helps to insulate you (whether you're hiking, sitting, or fast asleep). Still cold? Wear a hat, extra socks, and gloves.
- Sip a hot drink before bed and use the leftovers as a hot-water bottle.

Self-inflating Mattresses.

Q. My air mattress is supposed to be self-inflatable, but it doesn't seem to be. Is it defective?

A. Probably not. You can't just open the valve and hop on top of the mattress. Self-inflation takes time. Smaller, thinner mattresses self-inflate more quickly than the thick, cushy ones (which need more air). And no air mattress *completely* self-inflates—that would be scientifically impossible. You always

After the mattress self-inflates, give a few puffs of air to finish off the job.

need to add a few puffs of air so that there's more air pressure inside the mattress than outside it.

Self-deflating Mattress?

Q. On a recent winter trip, my air mattress seemed fine when I blew it up, but before I even went to bed, it was limp. I checked at home, but there doesn't seem to be a leak. What's wrong with it?

A. In a word, physics. Since you blew up your air mattress rather than letting it self-inflate, you put 98.6-degree air into it. While you ate dinner and hung around camp, the air in the mattress naturally started to cool. As air cools, it takes up less volume. That's why the mattress felt like it lost air. When this happens on a cold night, all you have to do is add a few more puffs.

Clothing

Staying Warm.

Q. What clothes should I take for a three-season mountain hike where I don't know what the weather will be like?

A. Taking several layers of lightweight insulating clothing gives you the ability to mix and match your clothes to fit changing conditions. Except in the dead of winter or on a major climb, I rarely take anything so bulky as a down jacket. I'm much more likely to take a synthetic long-sleeved shirt, a light fleece shirt, and perhaps a heavier fleece jacket or vest, which can be combined in a variety of ways. Layering also keeps you warmer because it traps air more effectively between different layers of clothing, and it allows you to avoid overheating. If you start working up a sweat, you simply remove some clothes.

Dead Man's Clothing?

Q. Is cotton really so bad? If so, why do cowboys and other people who spend a lot of time outdoors wear blue jeans?

A. Anyone who has been reading up on hiking clothing anytime during the last 20 years has probably heard the mantra "Cotton kills!"

As you pointed out, cotton has a traditional place in the great outdoors. After all, blue jeans were invented for gold miners, and cowboys wouldn't be caught dead in synthetic polyester pants!

But we backpackers have to sleep with our mistakes—and carry them, too. For us, cotton is an all-round bad idea. It absorbs sweat. It doesn't wick away moisture; it holds moisture right up against the skin (which can cause rashes). It doesn't keep you warm when you're wet (in fact, having cold, wet cloth next to your skin actually causes you to chill faster). And cotton takes a long time to dry when you wash it.

Some hikers do wear cotton shirts and shorts in hot weather, especially in deserts, where there's next to no chance of a soaking rain. But even in deserts, many hikers prefer wicking synthetic fabrics. As a rule, there's no surer way to spot a novice on a trail than by a pair of blue jeans—no matter how worn they may be.

Hiking Shirts.

Q. What kind of shirt should I wear when hiking? Does it really make a difference?

A. The kind of shirt you wear while hiking is probably not the most important backpacking decision you'll make, especially in temperate weather, so I wouldn't sweat this one (pun intended) too much.

My favorite hiking shirt is a polyester mesh shirt that looks like a football jersey. The holes provide ventilation and moisture transfer, and the shirt doesn't look as ratty as a cotton T-shirt after a few hundred trail miles.

Polypropylene is another good all-around outdoor fabric because it wicks moisture away from your body. And it's very cheap. It has two drawbacks: You can't put polypropylene in a clothes dryer (it'll literally disintegrate), and after a couple of days of use it starts to stink. Since you sweat less when you sleep, polypro makes more sense as nighttime wear.

Other hikers use proprietary fabrics made by individual manufacturers. Some of these high-tech fabrics can go in a clothes drier and don't smell as bad as polypro—but they are considerably more expensive.

Cold-Weather Walking Clothes.

Q. What should I wear while hiking in winter? Long underwear? If so, what kind and what weight?

A. I use layers of synthetic moisture-wicking fabrics, which keep you warm and retain some insulating quality when wet. You can always throw your raingear over them if it snows or if you are cold. You don't have to be stuck with the "long-underwear" look. Some manufacturers make hiking tights with a more finished appearance.

Even in winter, you may find that you don't need much clothing while you're walking, because you're working hard. Everyone's body reacts a little differently to cold, but here are some guidelines.

In winter, you might want full waterproof/breathable coverage from head to toe (Appalachian Trail, New Jersey).

- Above 40 degrees: Shorts and a light long-sleeved shirt.
- In the 30s: Lightweight polypro long johns, long-sleeved shirt, fleece vest or wind jacket.
- In the 20s: Medium-weight polypro long johns and shirt; fleece vest, possibly add outer shell (pants and jacket).
- Below 20 degrees: Heavyweight polypro long johns; fleece jacket and/or outer shell (pants and jacket).
- Note that if the wind chill is significant, you need to add more layers. You also need more layers at night, when you're not working.
- To adjust the temperature when you start getting too hot or too cold, take off (or put on) hats and gloves.
- If you use thicker socks in winter, be sure your boots are big enough.

I Hate Bugs!

Q. I love everything about camping except for insects. How can I stay insect-free?

A. I'm not sure there's such a thing as being insect-free outdoors, but there are some ways to minimize the nuisance. I assume you already use a tent, not a tarp, with plenty of mosquito netting.

- Bring a bug suit. Loose-fitting long-sleeved shirts and lightweight long pants are definitely worth their weight during bug season. Mosquitoes easily bite through skin-tight polypropylene, but they can't get a grip on tightly woven, loose-fitting clothes. Light colors seem to repel them, as well. A head net is another option for the height of bug season.
- Choose a campsite high up. A windy knoll or a pass on dry, rocky ground is guaranteed to be less buggy than a meadow.
- Avoid camping near standing pools of water.
- Make a fire (if it is permitted) and let your clothes get very smoky.
- Use repellent. DEET is the standard, but old-time woodspeople swear that Avon's Skin-So-Soft lotion works against blackflies.
- Avoid bug season: The worst time of year to encounter insects is just after the spring snowmelt.

When to Pack a Hat.

Q. I'm going to be hiking in New England in July. Do I need to bring a warm hat?

A. If you'll be meandering through the gentle hills of northern Connecticut, I'd say no. If you're headed for New Hampshire's White Mountains, or Vermont's northern Green Mountains, or for above–tree line peaks in Maine, then yes, pack a hat just in case.

Here's a simple way to think about it: The reason an area is above tree line is that the climate is too severe for trees to survive. If the climate is too severe for trees, it's too severe for hatless heads! Remember: In most mountains that rise above tree line, it can snow any day of the year. Mountain weather can turn foul unpredictably and sometimes instantly. If you're going high, you need a hat. Make sure yours has a strap, or a gust of wind might steal it away.

Raingear: To Skimp or to Splurge?

Q. I'm in the market for new raingear. Do I really need to spend $300 on a jacket? I mostly hike in the summer in good weather, and it seems a real waste to spend that much money on something I almost never need.

In Washington's North Cascades the raingear you need is the best raingear you can afford. A pack cover comes in handy, too.

A. It's always a good idea to have raingear, even if you don't think you'll need it. It's nothing short of mind-boggling how quickly a hot summer sun can give way to a chilling rain.

But you're right to question whether you need highly engineered waterproof breathable fabrics for a summer weekend in the woods—especially since many of these fabrics don't ventilate that well in hot, humid weather. An inexpensive poncho costs a small fraction—and may even keep you more comfortable in warm weather because it's fully breathable. And it covers your pack, too!

Some inexpensive brands of raingear are also worth a look. Coated nylon doesn't breathe. Raingear made of this material allows air to circulate by means of vents; unfortunately, the pack straps can interfere with the vents. Some companies are coming out with inexpensive jackets and pants made of lightweight materials that don't wear well over the long haul, but may be the perfect solution for someone who wants a "just-in-case" layer should the unexpected happen.

Leaky Raingear.

Q. My Gore-Tex jacket used to keep me dry, but it doesn't anymore. Is there anything I can do?

A. Gore-Tex is a layer that is laminated to the inside of the nylon. There is also a repellency treatment on the outside of the nylon, which can deteriorate if it's dirty. When the repellency is shot, rain soaks the fabric, and you feel wet and cold, even though the water doesn't actually pass through the fabric. Condensation forms inside, so it appears that the garment is leaking.

You can rejuvenate your tired Gore-Tex by washing it in warm water in the gentle cycle with powdered detergent. Tumble dry, then treat with a water-repellency compound (available at an outfitter).

Boots

Day Hike Boots.

Q. I'm looking for waterproof, breathable mid-height boots suitable for day hiking. Any suggestions?

A. Just like in real estate, where the answer is always "location, location, location," with hiking boots, the answer is always "fit, fit, fit." The make and model are secondary.

Hikers' footwear ranges from running shoes to all-leather clod-hoppers and everything in between, as seen in this trekker's hut in New Zealand.

For backpacking, my preference is for lightweight fabric-and-leather boots with waterproof-breathable linings. These boots can handle a wide variety of terrain. If you get stuck in mud or snow, your feet will stay drier than they would with sneakers or trail shoes; if you have to navigate your way through rock and talus fields, your ankles will be better supported. And you get all that without the weight of a "traditional" all-leather hiking boot.

In my case, preference clashes with reality. I've tried many different brands and models, and the tragic fact is, none of them (so far) have been a perfect fit. So I always go back to my old reliable midweight leather hiking boots. They're heavier, but they fit.

For day hiking, you may not need a hiking boot at all. Backpackers use boots to help them support the heavy loads they carry. Day hikers don't have those heavy loads, so unless you're going to be tromping around in mud or navigating ankle-bending terrain, a trail shoe might be the ticket.

Boot Fitting.

Q. How do I tell if my boots fit right? In the store, they always seem to fit, but on the trail, I start getting blisters.

A. The traditional way of fitting boots is to:

▲ Try on boots in the later afternoon when your feet may be a little swollen.
▲ Wear hiking socks of the same thickness you would on the trail.
▲ Make sure there's plenty of room in the toebox by checking to see if the tips of your toes bang against the boot when you kick something or stand facing downhill on a ramp.
▲ Be sure your heels doesn't slide up too much when you stand facing uphill on the ramp and flex your ankles.

For some people, these simple tests aren't enough.

The first thing to ask is, where is your Achilles' heel? Do you, in fact, always get blisters on your heels? Or on your toes? Painful experience has taught me to ignore all the cool features of a boot until I ask one key question: Is there enough room for my little toe?

You might consider going to a store where personnel have been trained by boot-fitter Phil Oren. His exacting methods include looking at every detail of your foot: where you place your weight, how you step, whether you have a large-volume foot or a small-volume foot, whether and where you have other pedestrian idiosyncrasies with frightening names like pronation and supination. A list of dealers who perform this custom-fitting service can be found at *www.fitsystembyphiloren.com/ConDealers.html.*

Caring for your boots with a waterproofing compound can extend their life, but always check the manufacturer's recommendations (Manang, Nepal).

Boots: Your Mileage May Vary.

Q. How many miles can I expect to get out of a pair of boots? I've asked at stores, and I've even called the customer service reps at boot companies. No one will tell me.

A. That's because they can't.

Everyone walks differently—and everyone's boots show different signs of wear. Some people stomp straight through mud, puddles, and streams. Some people walk with balletic grace, delicately dancing among the rocks and roots. Some carry huge packs, some carry light ones. Some people coddle their boots, only hiking on gentle trails in good weather; others put them through an obstacle course worthy of boot camp. It also depends on what you consider worn-out. Do you retire your boots as soon as they show signs of wear, or do you wait until the sole has worn through and the stitching is splitting?

In the arcane world of long-distance hiking, people have studied everything from thru-hikers' caloric intake (4000–6000 calories a day) to their psychological profiles (long-distance hikers tend to be more introverted than the general population) to—yes—their boot mileage. The following figures are intended only as general averages. Your mileage, as they say, may vary.

Midweight all-leather boots: 1000–1500 miles

Lightweight leather-and-fabric boots: 800–1200 miles

Sneakers: 500–700 miles.

Too-Small Boots.

Q. Is there anything I can do about a pair of boots that is too small?

A. You could try wearing thinner socks (this could give you as much as one half size of difference in the fit).

You could also ask a cobbler to "stretch" them. (Tell him precisely where the boot is feeling tight.) Another thought: you could replace the removable insoles with a thinner variety.

If these tricks don't work, you're probably ready for a new pair.

Boots versus Sneakers.

Q. What's the deal with wearing sneakers on trails? Are boots really necessary?

A. Some people certainly think so. In recent years, it's been a trend to hike in sneakers or trail shoes on some long-distance trails. But it depends on you. If you're carrying a heavy pack on rough terrain, boots are the better choice because they offer more support (see "Ultralight Hiking," earlier in this chapter). If you're traveling light, and if the trails are well constructed and reasonably mud-free, then trail shoes or running shoes may be adequate.

Crampon Alternatives.

Q. I'm going to be hiking in the Rockies in June, and I hear I may have to cross snowfields and ice patches. Should I take crampons?

A. You probably don't need full-fledged crampons for June hiking, although it's best to check with the ranger station just before you leave for current conditions. An ice ax is a more useful tool. (If you don't know how to use it, take a class.)

For crossing spring and summer snow and ice slopes, I find four-prong instep crampons useful. These are small, lightweight mini-crampons that attach to the instep of almost any boot (although you might have to adjust them) and give you added traction on snow and ice. I've used them on Kilimanjaro and in California's High Sierra and recommend them highly for late-spring conditions.

For more on hiking and camping in snow and ice, see "Snow-free High Country," Chapter 2, and Chapter 6.

Miscellaneous Gear

Stoves and Fuel Availability.

Q. I'm planning a hike in Idaho and I think I'll need to replenish fuel at some point. Will I have trouble finding it?

A. Fuel for camp stoves is widely available in stores in and near many recreation areas. Propane-butane canisters can even be found in convenience stores (of course, that only helps if you're using a stove that accepts those canisters). White gas is usually available in outfitting stores and stores that cater to recreationists.

Multi-fuel stoves that take kerosene, unleaded auto gas, and white gas are especially convenient because if all else fails you can go to a gas station. Additionally, a few multi-fuel stoves run on both canisters and liquid fuel.

Stoves Abroad.

Q. I'm going on a round-the-world trip and I hope to backpack in Asia, Africa, and Europe. What kind of stove should I take?

A. Different kinds of fuel are more (or less) available in different countries. There are two strategies for foreign travel:

You could find out which are the most common fuels available and choose a stove that uses them. So if you were traveling in France, you would use one of the widely available French-made Camping Gaz stoves; in Nepal, you would use a stove that burns kerosene.

Or you could choose a stove that burns a wide variety of fuels. A stove that can handle white gas, unleaded automobile fuel, kerosene, white spirits, and petroleum-based dry cleaning fluid (commonly available in many different countries) will probably see you through most, if not all, situations. Don't count on being able to use unleaded gasoline from a gas station, though. In some countries, it's not available, and in other countries, gas stations will not sell small quantities of fuel to people on foot.

The Boiling Point.

Q. Why does it take so long for food to cook at higher elevations?

A. As a result of the lower air pressure at higher elevations, water boils at a lower temperature (approximately 1.8 degrees Fahrenheit for every 1000 feet). So, while at sea level water must reach 212 degrees before it boils, at 10,000 feet it must only reach 194 degrees. The time it takes to cook a pot of spaghetti depends on the heat; since the water is not as hot, the food must cook longer.

A windscreen increases your stove's efficiency.

Notice that this means cooking the same pot of spaghetti takes not only more time, but more fuel, too.

Stove Windscreens.

Q. Is it really worthwhile to carry those flimsy little windscreens that come with some stoves?

A. By keeping the wind from blowing the flame away from the pot, the windscreen makes your stove more efficient. True, you can use natural wind-breaks, like logs and rocks. But a windscreen keeps the heat right next to the pot. It reduces the amount of fuel you have to use—and it makes cooking quicker, too.

Packing a Camera.

Q. I love to take pictures, but I hate having to stop, put down my pack, take out the camera, take the photo, put the camera back, and load up again. Is there a better way?

A. Fortunately, yes.

If you're going to get good shots, the camera has got to be handy. Hikers who are serious about their pictures carry their cameras where they can get at them—it doesn't matter if it's a tiny digital point-and-shoot or a massive SLR with a telephoto lens. If the former, you can tuck it into a pouch hung from your hipbelt. If the latter, a case that rests on your chest is the best solution. These cases come with harnesses that strap around your back. The harness keeps the camera from bouncing against your chest and distributes most of its weight around your back so your neck doesn't get sore. The case keeps it protected from dirt and rain (although, note that while most of these cases offer protection from rain, they are *not* fully waterproof; see below.)

For more on carrying cameras, see "Lugging Camera Gear," Chapter 5.

Waterproofing Cameras.

Q. I hike in conditions that are frequently quite wet. How do I keep my camera dry?

A. Good question, since most camera cases—even those you will buy at an outfitting store—are *not* waterproof. Here are some solutions:

▲ Line the camera case with a plastic zipper-lock bag—and use it.
▲ Buy a "dry bag" designed for kayakers.
▲ Get a waterproof camera. This is an expensive solution, but no more expensive than ruining a camera in the rain. Using a waterproof camera allows you to actually take pictures in the middle of a full-fledged deluge—something you can't do with a regular camera, no matter how you're carrying it.

A chest pack for your camera distributes its weight more comfortably and keeps the camera close at hand.

Two poles help the author keep her balance while crossing a stream.

Benefits of Walking Sticks.

Q. I've read a lot of what sounds like hype about walking sticks. Do trekking poles really help that much? Why can't I just use a stick I find in the woods?

A. Trekking poles are becoming more and more popular. Here's why:
Walking sticks transfer some of the pressure from your knees and leg

muscles to your arms. This is especially important on steep trails, where your knees take a beating—a potentially serious problem for older hikers and also for hikers who are overweight.

Telescoping trekking poles are easier to take on planes and can be shortened to support a tarp at night. Poles with shock-absorbing springs have some "give" to them. When you hop down from a boulder to the ground, the springs absorb some of the shock that would otherwise land on your knees. (See Chapter 9 for other knee-saving strategies.)

A residual benefit of trekking poles is that they give your hands something to do: Many hikers find that their fingers swell in hot weather. Gripping the poles seems to keep the circulation going and the swelling down.

But there's nothing wrong with using a traditional hiking staff. I've used a broom handle, a discarded ski area boundary marker, a dead stalk from a century plant, and dozens of sticks I've picked off the forest floor.

Two Poles or One?

Q. What's the deal with two poles? Is this just a trend? Or is there actual value in using two poles instead of one?

A. It's a matter of personal preference. I use two walking sticks, not one, because I like the rhythm of walking with two poles. A friend of mine who is a park service ranger feels that two poles completely throw off her balance. Some people find that it takes a while to get used to using two sticks, but once they do, they can't imagine hiking any other way. So try both and do what works.

An advantage to using one pole is that you have your other hand free to do things like adjust your pack straps, drink some water, or scratch a mosquito bite. The advantage to using two poles: Better support when you have to take giant downhill steps; you can support your weight by leaning on both hands. Using two poles also puts your arms to work, making it a little easier to propel yourself uphill.

Stuff Sacks.

Q. Why should I spend money on stuff sacks? Can't I just use garbage bags?

A. Yes, you could, although garbage bags on their own will soon start to tear.

Stuff sacks offer some advantages. First: Color. By buying sacks in a variety of different colors, you won't end up rummaging through the red bag that holds your sleeping bag when you really want the red bag that holds your clothes. Stuff sacks also come in different shapes and sizes, which makes packing easier.

Waterproof stuff sacks are a good idea for sleeping bags and warm clothing. You could, however, also line a regular stuff sack with a garbage bag or a large plastic freezer bag.

Finally, stuff sacks with compression straps are useful for bulky items like winter sleeping bags and winter clothes.

Stuffing and Packing.

Q. I can't seem to fit my sleeping bag into the stuff sack it came in. Do I have to roll it up every time I pack it? I have the same problem with my tent. Should I fold it?

A. The first thing I do when I get a tent (or a sleeping bag) is trade up to a slightly larger stuff sack. The sacks that come with a product are usually fitted very tightly. Why hassle with a stuff sack that barely fits?

As for rolling and folding, there's a reason why they call them *stuff* sacks! Stuffing is easier. It also prevents tent fabrics from developing weak spots in the places where they have been folded time and again.

Chapter 5

Stepping Out
BACKPACKING AND TRAIL TECHNIQUES

When I started writing hiking books, it amazed me that there was so much to talk about. I mean, backpacking is just walking with some stuff on your back, right? Well, not exactly. There are plenty of skills to learn that will help you be a better, more comfortable outdoorsperson.

The questions people ask about hiking know-how fall into several basic categories, including mileage, routefinding and navigation, right-of-way, packing, and hauling. They cover everything from figuring out your daily mileage to using the "rest step."

Mileage

Hiking Times.

Q. How do you know how long it will take you to hike certain lengths of trail? For example, if there is a trail that is 65 miles long, how long does it take to hike it?

A. The first factor to consider is your fitness. Don't lie to yourself, because your body is going to confront you with the truth once you get out on the trail! (Chapter 9 offers suggestions about off-season and pre-hike training.)

A few averages are useful as a starting point. Most backpackers carrying a full load hike at about 2 to 2½ miles per hour over the course of a day. For most people 8 to 10 miles a day is plenty, because you also need to factor in time for rests, lunch, photos, views, and snacks. However, long-distance hikers and others who are extremely fit walk a great deal faster and often cover more than double that mileage. For average hikers, add in an extra half hour for every 1000 feet of elevation gain. Depending on your personal ratio of logging miles to lollygagging, and depending on the terrain, it could take you as little as 3 hours to cover that 8–10-mile distance—or it could take all day. I'd suggest you go on a couple of weekend hikes and see what you're comfortable with. You'll soon get a sense for what you can do.

Even when you get a sense of your mileage, there are variables that will affect how far you can travel in day. First of all, the trail: A mountain traverse over steep ice slopes with 4000-foot climbs is going to take a *lot* longer than a flat path that could double as a bowling alley (see below). Another issue is footway: Are you walking on a smooth surface or on rocky glacial debris? Are there challenges like stream fords and navigational difficulties? The best way to find out about specific trail conditions is to check a guidebook.

Note that some guidebooks may suggest a certain number of days to do a

On difficult trails, such as this section of New Hampshire's Appalachian Trail, hikers are lucky to cover a mile an hour.

On well-marked and well-graded trails, such as this stretch of the Pacific Crest Trail, many hikers walk at a pace of 3 miles an hour or even more.

trail or a stretch of trail. Sometimes, these suggestions may seem odd. Often, the suggestions reflect anomalies in the trail: Perhaps it's a very difficult stretch ' with a tough climb over a high pass, and even the most fit and experienced hikers can't do big mileage there. Perhaps there's very little water, and hikers must cover larger-than-average distances to camp near a water source. Or perhaps it's in a national park or a state park where campsites are fixed and rigid. If the mileage recommended by a guidebook seems a little weird to you, ask the land management agency or the trail-maintaining club about it.

Mountain Mileage.

Q. My friend and I are coming over from Scotland to walk the John Muir Trail. We have planned an average daily mileage of 14 miles, based on the mileage we cover at home. However, we do not know anyone who has traveled in this area before, so we are unfamiliar with the terrain. Could you give us some information regarding this estimate?

A. You're right to ask about this. Mountain mileage is different than valley and forest mileage, especially if you have to deal with snow.

Mountain mileage depends on terrain, steepness, trail quality, heat, water availability, as well as your fitness and how much weight you are carrying in your pack. There's quite a bit of climbing and descending on the John Muir Trail because the route of travel goes against the grain of the High Sierra range. Whenever you're gaining and losing 3000 or more feet at a time, you've got to figure that your mileage is going to plummet.

On mountain trails, you also have to contend with the effects of altitude. The JMT, along with many trails in Colorado and California, varies between about 9000 and 13,000 feet. At that height, you can be affected by altitude sickness (see Chapter 9). Even if the altitude doesn't make you sick, it might make you slow.

Snow is another issue. In most American mountain ranges, snow melts completely by the first or second week in July—unless it's been an unusually snowy winter. In rare cases, the higher elevations of mountains like the Sierra Nevada, the Colorado Rockies, and the North Cascades can be snow-covered all summer long!

I've hiked the Sierra three times—in June, July, and August—and each hike was a very different experience. In June, the higher elevations were covered with snow for miles at a time. In July and August the trail was much easier, but even so, the elevation changes and the long ups and downs made for difficult days. My mileage averaged about 15 miles a day on all three trips, but those miles were much more difficult to cover in June than in August. No matter what the conditions, in high mountains with numerous

In high mountains, mileage and pace may decrease because of obstacles like snowfields.

ascents and descent, 15 miles a day is ambitious. A very motivated, fit, and experienced hiker would be able to cover that distance, but more leisurely or less experienced folks would be better off with 8–10 miles a day.

Measuring Map Miles.

Q. When I'm looking at a trail on a map, how can I tell how many miles it is from one point to the next?

A. With practice, you can develop the skill to look at a map and count off the trail miles. It is possible to be quite accurate—if you are careful to take into account swiggles and switchbacks.

To be more accurate with less work, you can use a little device called a measuring wheel, which is available at some outfitting stores and map dealers. It can be adjusted to fit different map scales. You simply run it carefully over your intended route, and it converts map inches (or centimeters) to walking miles (or kilometers).

When using a wheel, you should probably add 10–20 percent to the estimated mileage, depending on the terrain and the scale of the map. First, the map wheel cannot measure changes in elevation. An up-and-down route (look for contour lines gathered close together) covers more miles than a flat route. And second, there are always more twists and turns than the map can show (which add up to more mileage). The smaller the scale of the map, the less detail it can include, and the less accurate your measurements will be.

A new tool on the market is map software, which can tell you the precise length of marked trails (after you enter several waypoints to mark the twists and turns, ups and downs), along with a ton of other useful information. The learning curve for these products can seem quite steep to technology neophytes. Digital map kiosks at outdoor retailers are a good place to investigate these products.

Walking Uphill.

Q. No matter how much hiking I do, I can't seem to get the knack of going uphill. I always feel like I have to gasp from tree to tree. Am I doing something wrong?

A. Assuming that there's nothing wrong with your heart and lungs other than perhaps being a little out of shape, it's very likely that you're not climbing in the most efficient way. A majority of people hike exactly as you described—pushing themselves from tree to tree until they collapse in a heap.

Map mileage is likely to understate the real distance because few measuring devices can accurately account for switchbacks like these (Sierra Buttes, California).

Fortunately, there is a better way.

The "rest step" technique forces you to slow down and take a tiny break between each step. Basically, it allows you to find a pace—however slow—that you can stick with all day. The rest step momentarily takes pressure off your muscles and puts it on your skeletal system. It also forces you to walk in a rhythm so you don't start speeding up beyond what's sustainable.

Here's how it's done: Take a step and then pause just as your uphill foot moves into place. Your back leg is straight, and the weight is still on it. Then, transfer the weight to your uphill foot. Take the next step. Pause again. Keep stepping and resting and stepping and resting—all the way up!

Routefinding

Staying Found.

Q. I recently found myself lost on a trail after taking the wrong fork. Fortunately, someone came along and pointed me in the right direction, because I was completed turned around! Why does this happen, and how can I prevent it?

A. Perhaps we "civilized" folk have lost our natural sense of navigation because so many of us live on a grid of straight-line streets that run at right angles to other straight-line streets. We've seemingly lost our ability to keep track of our direction when we follow gently twisting and turning trails. But that's just a theory.

Getting lost is usually the result of one of three things: not paying attention, poor navigation skills, or refusing to believe we've made a mistake. One of the easiest ways to get lost is to rely on a sense of direction that isn't as well-developed as it should be! Instead, take frequent compass bearings and pay attention to natural direction signs like the position of the sun and shadows at different times of day.

Another way we get lost is that we assume that because there is a trail under our feet, it is the *right* trail. This is the "fallacy of the expected": a fallacy that assures us that we are where we are supposed to be because we expect to be there.

Before you start hiking, look closely at the map. What major landmarks should you expect to see, and how long should it take you to get from one to the next? What trail junctions should you watch for? You need to see these landmarks in your mind and tick them off as you go. If you encounter something you weren't expecting to see, or if the compass says you are going south and the map says you should be walking east, you need to stop and reconcile those discrepancies, the sooner the better.

All that said, some people do have problems learning to navigate. A hands-on class offered by a hiking club or an outdoor store may be just the ticket. You can practice in an area close to home. Or try the increasingly popular sport of orienteering, which combines an old-fashioned foot-race with map-reading, navigating, and map-and-compass work.

Getting Unlost.

Q. What do I do if I get lost?

A. Just because you've lost your way is no reason to lose your head. In fact, the best way to find your way is to keep your wits about you. Just as most people become lost by the "fallacy of the expected" (see above), most people exacerbate the problem by pushing on in a half-panic, leaving their wits scattered all over the (wrong) trail. Looking back on the experience of being lost after the fact, many hikers are stunned to realize how soon they knew at a gut level that they weren't quite where they should be—and at how long it took them to let this knowledge travel from gut to brain, ignoring such evidence as the fact that the sun was setting in the wrong part of the sky.

The best thing to do as you're hiking is to constantly reconcile the terrain

Part of staying found is stopping to check your location against the map. Consult your hiking partner: two heads are better than one.

with the map. If you determine that the map and the ground are sending different information to your brain, it's time to stop and evaluate the situation. If you've been diligent, you've probably not gone too far out of your way. Try to locate landmarks on the terrain and match them to your map. Remember the last time you absolutely knew where you were, and try to reconstruct what you've done since then. Do not let your evil ego try to convince you that you are where you are supposed to be. If the map says you are supposed to be on top of a mountain and you are sitting on a valley floor, something has gone wrong, and you need to fix it. Instead, look at the map. Could you possibly have missed the turn at a trail junction?

Usually, some calm mental work is all it will take to get you back on track. But if you are truly lost, two strategies should eventually get you found again. First, you can follow a river downstream—easier said than done, and a strategy to be used only in the most dire of emergencies. "Downstream" will always ultimately lead somewhere—but it may take forever to get there, and it may be somewhere completely different than you wanted to be. Better, you can estimate your approximate location on the map (you're on foot— you probably haven't walked *that* far out of your way), and then choose a compass bearing that will eventually intersect with a prominent feature like a trail or a ridge. Follow the bearing religiously; when you get to the feature, you'll have one incontrovertible landmark, and you can use basic map and compass skills to identify other landmarks and find your position. (This is called triangulating; for details, consult a map-and-compass book like Bjorn Kjellstrom's *Be Expert with Map and Compass*.)

Note that a GPS unit completely eliminates this problem because it gives you latitude and longitude coordinates that tell you exactly where you are. Basic map-reading skills are then still required to use this information to find the trail and your proper direction.

GPS.

Q. Is a GPS unit a necessary supplement to a compass and maps? Would you carry one for an entire thru-hike? What are some of the pros and cons?

A. This is the kind of question that makes me feel like an old grandma. You know: "When I was a kid we had to hike barefoot through the snow because they hadn't invented leather yet."

I don't know if GPS even existed when I started backpacking. If it did, it certainly wasn't available to backpackers. If you were going to hike, you had to know how to use a map and compass.

But time—and technology—marches on. Today, GPS units are cheaper than ever, and more accurate, too.

Basically, you need to be able to do two things when navigating: identify your location, and plot a route. GPS is great for identifying your location. It can pinpoint where you are within a few feet. Plotting a route is trickier. A GPS unit can tell you which way is north, or northeast, or whatever (just like a compass). But you still need to be able to read a map well enough to plot a path that works with the contours and particularities of the landscape. A GPS can't help with that unless you first take the time to program it with the precise waypoints of your route. Even then, the information in the device may not be detailed enough to help when you're on tricky terrain in bad visibility.

I confess to being old-fashioned enough to take pleasure in being able to use a map and compass. And I take comfort in the knowledge that even if my GPS batteries run out, or the device gets drowned in a storm, or I fall on it and smash it, I can still use my low-tech skills to keep going. GPS isn't a substitute for knowing how to use a map and compass, but it's a useful tool on unmarked trails and when traveling cross-country. I wouldn't bother with it on well-blazed trails, though.

Blazing a Trail.

Q. We're trying to clean up a county park that has been over-blazed. How far apart should the blazes on the trees be? How large should they be? If I can come up with some guidelines, I'll have a better chance of getting the place properly and unobtrusively marked.

A. By even trying to answer this one, I'm diving into a sea of controversy. Some hikers want blazes on just about every tree. Many wilderness managers feel that in wilderness areas, trails should only be marked at junctions. On some trails you can walk for miles without seeing any blazes at all.

Trails in county parks such as you describe are usually obviously blazed because users may not have good navigation skills.

There are several ways to mark trails: paint blazes; cairns (piles of stone, sometimes called ducks); markers made of wood, metal, or plastic; or ax blazes cut into trees. On the Appalachian Trail, white blazes are 6 inches high and 2 inches wide, whenever possible at eye level. In the West, ax blazes are more common.

One common standard is to mark trails so that each blaze is just visible from the next. If the footway is very obvious, blazes can be a little farther apart; if it's not obvious, then you'll want the blazes closer together. You don't want to paint every single tree—but you don't want to have to keep sending out search parties, either. A change of direction is often indicated by doubling the blazes.

In dealing with over-blazing, you can "brown out" (paint over) some of the blazes that are too close together. Once you've done that, walk the trail and try to determine where else blazes might be needed. The best way to double-check your work is to hike with someone who does not know the trail. When they get confused, that's where you need a blaze. Be sure that the trail is blazed in both directions, and test-hike it both ways. Try to imagine the conditions in fog or snow, when the trail might be obscured.

For more information, check out *The Complete Guide to Trail Building and Maintenance,* by Carl Demrow and David Salisbury.

Right-of-Way

Rules of the Road.

Q. Who yields the right-of-way on trails, the person going uphill or down?

A. I'm of the opinion that the fewer authoritatively stated "rules" we have, the better. I'd much rather step aside and exchange a pleasant hello than argue about who has the right-of-way. No organization that I know of has a policy on the right-of-way among hikers—uphill, downhill, or flat.

Common sense should prevail. Most responsible group leaders ask their members to yield to individual hikers. Groups can have a huge impact in the wilderness, and this kind of politesse goes a long way toward making everyone's backcountry experience more pleasant.

As far as the uphill-downhill thing is concerned, when I'm hiking uphill, I usually don't mind pausing to take an extra gulp of air to let someone going downhill get past. But if you're scampering downhill, and you see someone laboring uphill trying to maintain a rhythm, why not cut her some slack and step off the trail?

I guess the bottom line is, if you think you're stepping off the trail too often, try a different (less crowded) trail. Honestly, in 17,000 miles or so of hiking, I've never found this to be an issue.

Horses and Right-of-Way.

Q. Why do horseback riders have the right-of-way? They're just sitting there. Why can't they let us go past?

A. On multiple-use trails, hikers have the right-of-way over bicyclists and horseback riders have the right-of-way over anyone else.

The reason that equestrians (and other stock users) have the right-of-way is that they are sitting on top of a 1000-plus-pound animal that can be skit-

Livestock gets the right-of-way. Why? It's easier for you to move than for them to move.

tish, nervous, or just plain ornery. It's much easier for a hiker to step off a trail than it is for a rider—and it does less damage to the trail.

Many people who ride on trails (especially those in groups led by commercial outfitters) have very little control over their mounts. Novice riders are unlikely to be able to make their horses move off a trail; you may as well ask them to make those horses jump to the moon. Also, horses are often spooked by the sight of people wearing packs.

When you see a group of riders approaching, be prepared to stand well off the trail and do what the leader tells you. It's in the interest of safety—theirs *and* yours.

Managing Your Load

Hauling Water.

Q. I'm going to be hiking in Arizona's Sonoran Desert. How do I carry 5 or 6 liters of water?

A. Look on the bright side—you only have to carry all that water until you take your first sip! After that, you will have to carry a little less, and a little less, and a little less—until it's time to start wishing you were carrying more again.

For packing water: I use fabric water bags, which are more flexible for packing than hard bottles. I use two or three small bags in order to balance the weight better; also, in the unlikely event that a bag springs a leak, I won't lose all my water! I choose bags with very secure closures and tough fabric that can withstand the occasional collision with a cactus. (But take duct tape, just in case. . . .) Water is heavy, so most hikers find that they are more comfortable if it is carried high and as close to the back as possible, following pack manufacturers' recommendations.

How Much Water?

Q. I'm headed for the PCT in southern California. How do I know exactly how much water to carry?

A. How much water you carry depends on the mileage between water sources, the elevation gain, the temperature, your fitness, the likelihood of finding water en route, and information on current conditions (available on the PCT from the Pacific Crest Trail Association).

Studies done for the U.S. military show that people engaged in active labor in hot weather lose as much as 1 to 1½ liters of water per hour because of perspiration. Endurance athletes may sweat up to 2 liters of water per hour. If you're hiking for 20 miles between water sources, and if you hike at an average pace of 2½ miles an hour, you would need a minimum of 8 liters (and maybe as much as 12 liters!) to replace all the water you sweated away. However, that doesn't mean you need to carry 8 liters. Drink up before you start walking, ration your water as you go, and replenish it when you reach the next water source.

Assuming the above example (20 miles between water sources, hot weather, endless ups and downs), you'll probably need to carry at least 4 or 5 liters of water in between. On the PCT I carried up to 7 liters of water on long, dry stretches in very hot weather. You need more water if you intend to camp where there is no water source. As hikers break in, their bodies usually

A sturdy water bag lets you carry as much water as you need without worrying (too much) about spillage.

become more efficient and need less water. Out-of-shape hikers need more water. (For more on hydration and health, see Chapter 9.)

Packing Right.

Q. Is there one right way to pack a backpack? Should the tent be inside the pack, or tied on the outside? Should the sleeping bag be rolled up and tied on the outside or kept on the inside? Please help a beginner and go from start to finish.

A. There's no single "right" way to pack a backpack. How you pack depends on your gear and how it all fits together. A hefty three-person tent takes more

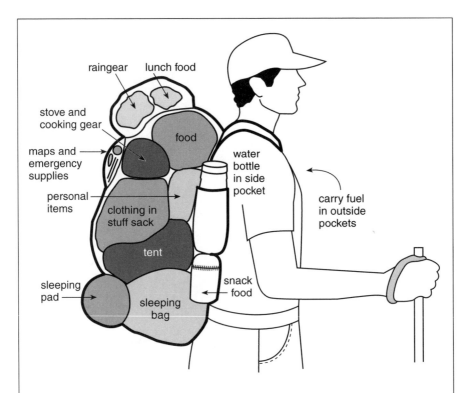

raingear   lunch food

stove and
cooking gear

food

maps and
emergency
supplies

water
bottle
in side
pocket

personal
items

carry fuel
in outside
pockets

clothing in
stuff sack

tent

sleeping
pad

snack
food

sleeping
bag

Pack Like a Pro

At 40 pounds, a fully loaded backpack can wear you down or strain your back if not loaded correctly. Packing smart starts with a good fit. Have your outdoor retailer fine-tune the strap adjustments for your torso and expected load.

Consider the terrain, too: On level ground, put the weight up high and cinch the pack in close to your back; on boulders and through rough brush, relocate weight low to help your balance. Always distribute weight equally side to side.

▲ Water, snacks, fuel, maps, guidebook, flashlight, pocketknife, first-aid kit, raingear, pack cover, and other emergency supplies all go in external pockets.

▲ Food (your heaviest category) rides high and close to the body. Cooking gear below that for convenience.

▲ Clothing deep inside, in stuff sacks or sealable plastic bags.

▲ Sleeping bag inside lowest compartment.

▲ Sleeping pad, inside plastic bag, strapped on outside, high or low as you like.

▲ Depending on the configuration of your pack and the weather, the tent can go inside or outside.

▲ Color coding your stuff sacks, memorizing your packing plan, and sticking to it will eliminate confusion about where items are stored.

space than a smaller tarp. If you have a small pack, you may have to strap things on the outside.

Most packs are designed to be comfortable when the load rides high, so as a rule you should pack lighter gear near the bottom and heavier gear higher up. Some people (especially women) prefer to carry the bulk of the weight lower on their bodies. You may feel more sure-footed if you carry the weight down low when you're going off-trail or have to scramble.

Most internal-frame packs have separate compartments at the bottom for sleeping bags. External-frame packs usually have an obvious spot for the sleeping bag outside the pack or in a compartment at the bottom. If the sleeping bag rides outside, protect it in an absolutely fail-safe waterproof stuff sack.

There may be times when you want to move things around. For example, when I'm expecting bad weather, I pack the tent where the sleeping bag is "supposed" to go. This way, I can get to the tent fast without opening the rest of my pack in the middle of a downpour. Also, storing a wet tent in its own compartment segregates it from other gear.

Try to keep things that you might need during the day—raingear, mosquito repellent, water bottles, sunscreen, snacks, lunch—in a place that's easy to get to. I use outside compartments and a pouch that rides in front on the hipbelt.

Stoves, cooking gear, food, and other heavy items go up, and near your back. If you feel that these hard items are poking you in the back, you can use clothing to pad them.

Don't forget the most important thing of all: Before you start packing anything, make sure you really need every single item you intend to put in that pack.

Out of Space.

Q. I always seem to have more stuff than I can squeeze into my pack. What's the best way to strap stuff to the outside?

A. Different packs come with different kinds and numbers of outside straps. Start with what your pack already has.

If your pack doesn't have many straps and daisy-chains (rows of webbing loops), buy a few bungee cords. They come in sizes ranging from a few inches to more than a foot long. They can be used to strap on a pair of snowshoes, hold drying socks in place, or secure an air mattress. The only problem with bungees is that you have to keep an eye on them: They can develop a habit of disappearing into the dirt and grass around a campsite.

With internal-frame packs, you can also often pack something large like a tent or an air mattress between the body of the pack and the hood of the pack, and keep it in place by strapping the hood tightly down.

Try to avoid hanging so many things from your pack that you look (and sound) like a traveling tinker! Heavy gear hanging from your pack can affect your sense of balance. Plus, gear riding outside of your pack can get lost or may become damaged if it is scraped against trees or rocks. It's best to keep as many things inside the pack as possible—especially on terrain where you might have to do a little scrambling.

Lugging Camera Gear.

Q. I like to take landscape photos. I need to reach my locations before sunrise or during sunset. Backpacking with both backpacking gear and camera gear is too heavy. What advice could you give me?

A. Professional photographers love those sunrise-sunset shots, not just for the low-angle light but because dawn and dusk are good times for spotting wildlife (see "Seeing Animals," Chapter 10). Many photographers hike in and out of their locations, sometimes in the dark, and photographic gear can indeed make for cumbersome backpacking.

To maximize your shooting time, car-camp as close as possible to the place you want to photograph. Get up early—even when it's still dark—then hike to the location. Or hike out in the evening, after you've finished shooting.

Hiking in dim light or in the dark poses a few safety concerns. Trails can look very different in the dark, so choose an area you're familiar with so you won't be surprised by a fork in the trail or a difficult rocky stretch. Be sure to leave yourself enough time to get where you're going before the "golden hour" begins; it takes longer to hike in the dark. Take a strong flashlight—not one of those teeny minis—or a headlamp, with extra batteries. You'll also need warm clothes, especially if you're shooting in an arid climate, where there can be a big difference between daytime and nighttime temperatures. Tell someone where you're going, on what trail, and when you expect to be back—and stick to your plan! It's not a bad idea to cajole a partner to come with you: among other things, they can provide companionship and help you haul your gear. But tell them to bring a book or something else that will keep them occupied if you spend 3 hours photographing a caterpillar or a tumbleweed.

Chapter 6

Snow and Ice
ALPINE CONDITIONS
AND WINTER CAMPING

Sooner or later, you may find yourself hankering for a hike in the middle of January. Or you may feel the urge to go for a mountain summit in June, before the snow melts.

The fact is, snow is no reason to stay inside. Indeed, remember how joyful a "snow-day" was when you were a kid? You may feel the same way as an adult.

But hiking's fourth season does require a little more: more gear, more skills, more attention.

Up Before Dawn.

Q. I'm planning to hike in Nepal, and I heard they wake you up in the middle of the night to start the ascent up the high pass on the Annapurna Circuit. Why? Isn't it safer to climb when you can see what you're doing?

A. You will be able to see well enough with all that snow reflecting every lumen of light from stars, moon, and headlamps.

So-called alpine starts are traditional on many major peaks. It sounds counterintuitive, but there are good reasons to climb big mountains at night, or at least very early in the morning.

So-called alpine starts maximize the chance of climbing (and descending) in good weather and while the snow is still stable.

The first is weather. Often, the weather at night on big mountains is bright and stable. Storms and clouds start to build with the heat of the day. High winds can also be a factor. Remember, climbing is not about reaching the summit; it's about getting back down again.

Second, snow conditions deteriorate as the day wears on. Snow starts to melt and get sticky, and forms unwieldly clumps that cling to your crampons. Conditions may become much more slippery. And on some mountains, both avalanche danger and rock-fall danger increase as the day wears on and snow starts to thaw.

Finally, there's the beauty of greeting sunrise from a high pass or summit, which, no matter which mountain you're on, is usually unforgettable.

Winter for the Snow-Challenged.

Q. I am from southern Georgia and, believe me, we don't see a lot of snow. What is the best advice for those of us who are unfamiliar with the white stuff but would like to "enjoy" a backpacking trip in the snow?

A. I'd start by choosing a fairly temperate climate. Virginia's Shenandoah National Park, sure. Wyoming's Grand Teton National Park, probably not.

In light snow—say, up to about 6 inches—there's no real problem, except that you might occasionally lose the trail for a bit. If the snow is deeper than about a foot, you might need snowshoes. Walking in snowshoes is not difficult, but it does take a lot of effort. How much effort depends on the depth and type of snow—in deep fluffy stuff, your daily mileage could plummet to 5 or 6 miles a day! So, tip number one: if you don't want to snowshoe, have a couple of backup destinations in mind in case the snow in your first-choice destination is too deep to hike in.

National parks can be great winter destinations. If the trails get too difficult, you can always use the roads as an easier alternative. Shenandoah National Park's Skyline Drive, for example, is unplowed in winter and runs the length of the park.

The other challenge is cold. Bring a zero- or 10-degree sleeping bag and several layers of warm clothes, including a hat, extra dry socks, heavy gloves for warmth, and lightweight gloves for camp chores. Your main job as a winter camper is to stay warm and dry. That means that you have to pay attention to your exertion during the day. If you find yourself working too hard and sweating too much, slow down or remove layers; otherwise the sweat will later cool and you'll get uncomfortably, dangerously chilled. Change into dry clothes as soon as you stop hiking. Remember—everything takes longer in winter, including cooking, setting up your camp, and getting ready to go again in the morning. When you pack food, choose easy-to-cook meals. And bring some soup and hot-drink mixes—you'll really appreciate them when you're cold and tired.

On the East Coast, you can make your life easier by choosing a trail with shelters. The Long Trail, the Northville–Lake Placid Trail, the Appalachian Trail, and other trails (see Chapter 2) have shelters located within an easy walk of each other. Shelters give you a dry, snow-free place to come home to at the end of the day.

The final winter challenge is routefinding. Guidebook maps may be adequate for trails in the summer, but even the best-marked trails can disappear

Introduce yourself to winter camping in moderate terrain. On the Appalachian Trail in the southern Appalachians, winters are mild, and shelters offer protection from the snow.

under snow (especially if they are marked with white blazes!). You need solid navigation skills to handle winter hiking; a good map and GPS will help you stay found.

Above all, beginning winter hikers should not go solo. Bring along a hiking partner for safety (and companionship).

How Can Snow Stop Me?

Q. I'm planning to day hike on Mount Rainier in early July and have been told that it's possible that there still might be snow on many of the trails at that time. Other than slipping and falling, what other hazards might the snow-covered trails produce?

A. Hiking on snow and ice can be a lot of fun. But it can also be frustrating, and potentially dangerous.

In late spring and early summer, you may encounter a hard, consolidated snowpack that is in the process of melting. Mount Rainier gets a *lot* of snow, and the information you've heard is dead-on right. Depending on the elevation at which you intend to hike, you can expect to see quite a bit in June and early July. In places, the snowpack may be several feet deep. (Note that on south-facing slopes and at lower elevations, snow melts earlier.) Here's how the white stuff can slow you down:

- **Slipping and sliding.** Even a light layer of snow can be hazardous, especially on trails strewn with obstacles like layers of fallen leaves, rocks, and roots. Steep, open slopes can present potentially life-threatening hazards, especially when the snowpack is subject to freezing, thawing, and rainfall. If you're traveling above tree line before the snow has melted, you should have an ice ax, and you should know how to use it.
- **Avalanches.** While more of a winter hazard than a spring hazard, avalanches do fall in the spring, especially after periods of variable and unstable weather (continuous thawing and refreezing), which weaken the snow. Ask at the ranger station about avalanche hazards on your route.
- **Navigation.** Snow can make a trail that is well marked and obvious in August impossible to find in June. When heavy construction has gone into trail building (blasting and switchbacks, for example), the route follows an imposed path, not a natural corridor of travel. These trails may be impossible to follow under snow because the constructed route is too steep and too exposed. You'll have to have the skills to find and follow your own route.
- **Snow depth and texture.** Spring snow is usually hard and consolidated, which makes it possible to walk on top of it, no matter how deep the snowpack. But late in the day, the crust softens (see "Walking on Suncups," below) and you can find yourself breaking through and having to "posthole," which is an exhausting way to get from point A to point B. You might also find yourself falling through snow that surrounds rocks because the rocks absorb more heat during the day and melt the snow around them. Unfortunately, snowshoes aren't much help in dealing with consolidated late-spring snow.
- **Stream crossings.** In June, many small and even large bridges may have been washed away by snowmelt. Snowmelt makes creeks and streams run faster and deeper. A crossing that barely tickles your toes in August may lap at your waist in June. Note: Trails may be snow-free at a lower elevations, but the creeks may still be flooded and dangerous to cross.
- **Sheer impassibility.** Sometimes the mountain just says no. Listen to it.

All that said, conditions on any major mountain vary from year to year. Check with rangers (preferably backcountry rangers with recent in-field experience) for local conditions. Be specific with your questions: Do you need

Hiking on snow not only takes more time, but it can be slippery and treacherous as well.

an ice ax? Is the trail you intend to hike passable? What about the river crossings? If the trail isn't passable, are alternate trails open?

Walking in Suncups.

Q. I've spent hours struggling in those saucer-shaped depressions in late-spring mountain snow. Any suggestions?

A. So-called suncups—saucer-shaped depressions that can be as deep as a bathtub—are the result of a combination of sunlight, solar radiation, heat, evaporation, dirt (which absorbs more heat than the surrounding snow), and wind. As temperatures rise during the day, suncups get deeper and more

Suncups are small—or large—depressions made when impurities in the snow absorb sunlight and the resulting heat melts into a cup. They can make for tedious walking.

pronounced. They can end up being quite jagged and nearly impossible to walk on. Suncups can be leveled by moist winds, but they re-form in periods of good weather.

Try to cross large patches of snow and ice early in the day. Later in the day, you might find yourself sinking through soft layers of snow all the way up to your thighs. Try to walk on harder, higher edges, which are less likely to break under your weight. They may challenge your balance; use hiking sticks or an ice ax for support.

Preventing Condensation.

Q. I have a zero-degree bag that keeps me snug even in mid-January. But in the morning, my tent is coated with frost that falls down and makes everything wet! How do I prevent condensation?

A. While you're sleeping, you're breathing and sweating, and all that breath and sweat has to go somewhere. Being hot, it rises, until it hits the cold tent fabric. Then it freezes into that fine layer of frost that falls on you in the morning.

Winter camping requires you to find a balance between ventilation and warmth. That's one reason why winter tents have ventilating flaps and windows. Having a little bit of air circulating helps narrow the temperature difference so warm air doesn't immediately freeze when it hits the tent fabric;

plus it gives the warm air a way to escape from the tent. Of course, if you have too much ventilation, all the warm air will escape, and you'll shiver all night. So you need to experiment, taking into account variables like the outside air temperature, the wind, and whether or not you have a hiking partner (more hot air, and I'm not talking about his political opinions). Using a vapor-barrier liner can also help by keeping your body heat (and moisture) close to your body; see also "Making a Bag Warmer," Chapter 4.

Sleeping in the Snow.

Q. Could give me some advice on pitching a tent in deep snow?

A. The trick is to make a solid surface on which to sleep. If you don't, the snow will simply collapse underneath you, and you'll end up sinking into it. Your body heat will melt some of the snow, your body weight will compress it, the snow will refreeze in lumps, and you'll end up sleeping on what will probably feel like a million ski moguls.

If the snow is deep enough to cause problems in the tent-pitching department, it's deep enough that you'd probably be traveling on snowshoes or skis. Either can be used to tamp down the snow and make a level, compact sleeping platform. You just stomp around until you have a good, hard snowpack underfoot. It's a great way to warm up at the end of the day.

Make your camping area quite a bit bigger than your tent, so you can also walk around outside. You also need to carve out an area for cooking. The bare-bones backcountry winter kitchen is just a flat area where you can walk or sit (don't sit directly on the snow; sit on a camping mattress to help prevent heat loss). You could indulge in a little snow architecture and sculpt a shelf on which to place your food and your stove. I also recommend tamping down a trail from the tent to your latrine pit, so that you can answer nature's call in the middle of the night without putting on snowshoes. When choosing your latrine area, remember to place it where the remains won't be obvious once the snow starts to melt.

Once you think you've compacted the snow as much as you can, give it a few minutes to settle and harden, then lay out your groundcloth and lie down for a test. If your "bed" doesn't feel solid, repeat the process.

Snow Stakes.

Q. How do you stake a tent in the snow? I tried to pitch my tent in the snow and the stakes kept popping out.

A. Those spindly little stakes that come with your three-season tent are fine for fields and forests, but they won't stay put in snow (or sand).

Special snow stakes are available. They are sort of shovel shaped, and have holes in them, and they get a much better grip. You can also make a so-called dead-man yourself by burying just about any object in the snow (not your hiking partner!) and tying off to it. One kind of dead-man is a commercially produced aluminum plate called a snow fluke, which is used both as an anchor in climbing and as a tent stake. Ski poles and skis can also make effective stakes.

Keeping Water from Freezing.

Q. I know I'm supposed to stay hydrated in winter, but when I wake up in the morning, my water is frozen! How can I prevent this?

A. Sleep with it. Yes, I'm serious.

Make sure you have a good water bottle with a strong seal. (No flimsy soda bottles in winter!) If you go to bed with a hot-water bottle, try to remember to open it after a couple of hours; otherwise, as the water chills, the bottle can start to contort from the change in temperature.

In less frigid temperatures, you can simply bring your water bags and bottles inside your tent, where the temperature will probably be above freezing. You can also bury the water bottle in the snow (which acts as an insulator). Bury it upside-down so that any ice forms at the bottom of the container and won't clog the mouth of the bottle. Just mark the place in the snow where you buried the water (perhaps with a ski pole or a snowshoe).

Winter Fires.

Q. I'm planning a winter hike. I like to have fires at the end of the day, especially in cold weather. How do you build a fire when there's snow on the ground?

A. Building a fire in the snow is a little trickier than in the middle of summer. Here are the basics:

Gather all your wood first. Organize pieces by size so that you'll have just the right stick when you need it.

Even wood buried under a layer of snow can be dry enough to burn, especially if the snow is the light and fluffy kind that has low moisture content. The worse the snow is for making snowballs, the better your chance of finding dry wood.

Break a stick to see if it's dry inside. If it cracks, it most likely is. However, if you're hiking after a winter rain, that crackling snap could be ice, from water that soaked through the wood and then froze. If that's the case, you'll need to look for dry wood in protected areas, like under thick vegetation or in the hollow of an old tree stump.

Try wood from different places around your site. Keep track of what wood you found where, so that if some of it goes up well and some of it simply smolders and smokes, you'll know where to return for more of the good stuff.

If the snow isn't too deep, dig a hole down to the ground. If the ground is covered with very deep snow, tamp down the snow where you want to make the fire so it's a solid, hard platform. (This will also form a depression, which will act as a windbreak.) Put a layer of wood down on the snow, and build the fire on that (otherwise, the fire will sink into the snow and go out before it even gets going). Wet or damp wood can take some time to get going; that's why firestarter is one of the Ten Essentials. You can buy firestarter at an outfitter, an army-navy store, or at convenience stores in many rural areas. Look for tubes of fire-ribbon, balls of wax mixed with sawdust, or tablets made of petroleum.

My favorite in-field trick is using laundry lint, which might be hanging around inside your pockets somewhere. Another quick fire-starting trick: If you have a little petroleum jelly or cooking oil and a cotton swab, apply the oil (or jelly) to the cotton swab and set it alight. You can also use old guide-book pages or the pages of that lousy paperback you've been toting along to read at night. Don't bother using toilet paper—it burns for only a second. Pine needles and birchbark are great fire starters. But don't rip birchbark off living trees—look for downed wood.

Don't forget your stove fuel: a dash of gas can give your fire the kick it needs to get going. For safety's sake, put the fuel on the fire before you light it, never after. Then toss in a match—and *stand back!*

When the fire is roaring, put any damp wood around it. The heat from the fire will dry it out, and you'll have a stash of dry wood for later, or for morning.

Chapter 7

A Woman's World
PERSONAL SAFETY,
HIKING PARTNERS, AND HYGIENE

In recent years, women have been among the fastest-growing group of outdoor enthusiasts. Most of the time, our questions are the same as those of our trail brethren. We want to know about gear, technique, where to hike, and what to eat. But some issues are unique to us.

But guys, wait! Don't flip past this chapter quite so fast. While issues of personal safety concern more women than men (and to a greater degree), men would be well advised to follow some of the suggestions in this chapter, including information ranging from whether to hike solo to whether to carry a gun. You may also benefit from the information on how to hike with a partner.

Personal Safety.

Q. I'd like to go backpacking, but I can't match my schedule with any organizations, groups, or friends. Being a city girl, I'm concerned about personal safety from unfriendly wildlife (human and non-human). Is it safe to hike alone?

A. I can tell you two things with confidence: One, no place on Earth is 100 percent safe; and two, the backcountry is probably a good deal safer than the city you call home.

Backcountry safety is something that any hiker, male or female, needs to consider when planning a hike, whether it's a day hike in a park or a thru-hike of a multi-thousand-mile trail. But as elsewhere in life, safety in the backcountry is a more pressing concern for women than it is for men.

Solo hiking offers many rewards, but it increases the risks inherent in any wilderness activity. In a tough spot, two people's judgment is often better than one person's. If one of you is injured, the other can perform first aid or go for help. If gear breaks, you might be able to share. Two people can offer each other moral support. Unless you are already an experienced outdoorsperson, it makes sense to have a partner.

If you do hike alone, here's what you can do on the trail to maximize your safety.

- ▲ Always let someone know when you're going and when you'll be back. Be as specific as possible about your route of travel and your intended campsites. Stick to the route you choose unless there are safety-related reasons to deviate, and tell your friends whom to call if you don't show up or call as planned.

- ▲ Check out your camping company. In an obviously popular campground or shelter, don't pitch your tent right away. Wait a while to see who shows up to be your neighbor. A Scout troop? Go ahead and camp. Three good ol' boys with a case of beer? Maybe it's time to "join your husband up the trail before he starts to worry." Don't tell strangers where you plan to camp. The "where ya been, where ya comin' from?" chit-chat is usually innocent—but keep it vague. If you feel uncomfortable, lie.

- ▲ If you feel uneasy about someone you've met on the trail, ask if they've seen your "husband" or the group you're with. Don't give out the info that you're hiking alone. And don't stick around with someone who gives you the creeps.

- ▲ Camp out of sight. I mean *really* out of sight. Go back to the trail and look to be sure your tent can't be seen.

- ▲ Carry a cell phone (see Chapter 8). Be aware that cell phones don't operate from just anywhere; they need a clear line of sight to a cell tower. If you can't get reception, climb a ridge and try again.

- ▲ Take a dog. (But see Chapter 10 for information about "Dogs in Bear Country.")

- ▲ Regarding wild animals, check local guidebooks to see what wildlife you might expect to encounter. Most wildlife keeps its distance from humans. You're more likely to be bothered by a mouse than a mountain lion! Most of the time, an animal that visits your campsite is looking for a free meal. Proper food storage is important. In bear country, check with the rangers for recommendations. Most bear problems involve improperly stored food.

Hiking with a partner offers company, a margin of safety—and someone to help hoist that bear bag!

See Chapter 10 for more suggestions on dealing with critters.

- ▲ Brush up on signaling skills. A whistle carries farther than a human voice; a mirror can be used to reflect sunlight and catch the attention of a rescuer.
- ▲ Take a first-aid kit-and know how to use it.
- ▲ For more health and safety concerns, see Chapter 9.

Weapons.

Q. I'm planning a solo hike, and I'm also a gun owner. Should I carry my gun with me?

A. This is one of the most controversial subjects in backpacking. Being a licensed and trained gun owner, you may indeed feel more secure with a firearm, and if you were indeed physically threatened or attacked by the one-in-a-million lunatic that occasionally wanders onto a trail, you might be thankful for the rest of your life that you had that weapon and the skill to use it at that moment. But you should realize that such occurrences are extremely rare, although not, unfortunately, unheard of.

You should also consider the other side of the argument:

▲ To be useful, a gun must be at hand and available—not stuffed in your pack, but in a holster. It will be visible to other hikers, which may intimidate them and color the nature of your interactions. Some people, especially parents with children, may choose to avoid you. Do you intend to carry it loaded? If so, you need to exercise triple the caution. If not, how useful will it be in a sudden emergency?

▲ Realize that there's not much a gun will protect you from. To be effective against a bear, you need a larger, more powerful weapon than you're probably thinking of carrying. No other animal is likely to be a threat to humans in the American backcountry (except, of course, another human).

▲ You must "babysit" your firearm at all times. You have to keep it with you (when you scamper up a hill for a view, when you go ¼ mile away to a spring—always).

▲ A firearm can be turned against you. Better to have a partner or a cell phone.

▲ Firearms are illegal in national parks and in many other areas.

Solo Thru-hiking.

Q. I want to thru-hike the Appalachian Trail. Is it safe to attempt a long-distance hike alone?

A. The safety concerns noted above all apply on the Appalachian Trail, as well as on other long-distance trails. Thru-hiking, after all, isn't much more than doing a week-long hike over and over (and over) again. There are a few additional considerations, however, for female long-distance hikers.

The Appalachian Trail is close to many small towns, and while the majority of interactions between locals and hikers are friendly, you might encounter a group of local yokels whose idea of a good time includes making overtures to you. Women have been harassed—and (very rarely) even attacked—on the AT. When hiking through areas that have reputations for being uncomfortable for women, remember that there is safety in numbers.

On any trail, be aware of the culture and the climate. America's small towns are usually paragons of hospitality and generosity, but this is not universally true, and women, especially women of color, can sometimes feel uncomfortable. Unlike in cities, it's common in small towns and rural area for strangers to say howdy and make conversation. You need to learn to differentiate between the common, friendly hello ("Hey stranger, why you walkin' in these parts?") and the "Hey baby" stuff that torments women throughout the world.

Resupplying is another problem for solo female hikers, because it occasionally involves hitchhiking into town. If you must hitchhike, it's always safer with a partner. If you have a cell phone, you could call a cab (if the town is big enough to have taxis) or make arrangements to be met at a trailhead by one of the many people who shuttle hikers around to trailheads. The Appalachian Trail Conference has a list.

You could try to find a hiking partner by advertising in trail club newsletters. On the AT, finding a partner is easy. More than 2000 people attempt a thru-hike of the trail each year, and the vast majority of them hike northbound starting in Georgia between March 15 and April 15. Quite often, hikers start alone, but then fall into loose associations and partnerships with other hikers. Some of these partnerships survive the entire trail. So don't fret if you don't find a hiking partner before your trip. Even if you don't find someone you want to hike with every day, you'll probably find plenty of company along the way.

Love on the Rocks?

Q. I love to hike and so does my fiancé. But it turns out we aren't exactly compatible hiking partners. He's much stronger than I am and he likes to do big miles, which I find debilitating. We were hoping to honeymoon on the Colorado Trail. Is this a good idea?

A. Well, it's harder to find a fiancé than a hiking partner, so I'd say it's worth working at.

As with all partnerships, a hiking partnership is about communication. It may be that you and your fiancé aren't 100 percent compatible for all hikes—very few people are. You need to talk about the character of each hike beforehand so that you are both clear about why you're going. If he wants a butt-busting bruiser of a hike, maybe it would be a good idea for you to sit that one out.

When you do hike together, expect to compromise during the day. It can be very frustrating for both the faster hiker and the slower hiker to have to try to walk at each other's pace. When the trail is obvious and clear, you might split up so you can each walk at the pace that is comfortable for you. The problem is that on remote, high trails (which are often not well marked), you might have to stick together so that you don't get lost or accidentally split up if one of you takes a wrong turn. If that's the case, Romeo could make it a little easier for you to keep up by taking on a little extra pack weight (after all, he wants a physical workout, right?).

Oh, and remember, the purpose of a honeymoon is to have together time—which means low mileage, lots of lazy mornings, and cozy isolated campsites.

Thru-hiking à Deux?

Q. I am an inexperienced backpacker planning to accompany my very experienced boyfriend on the entire Pacific Crest Trail. I'm *very* afraid of heights and snakes, and my biggest fear is steep, icy slopes. I don't want to slip and fall down a cliff to my death! Or cross raging waters by tightrope! *Please* tell me this won't be the case! Can I do this? I'm walking on my lunch hour every day, and will hike and backpack each very weekend until we leave. My boyfriend has hiked many sections of the PCT and this is his dream. Won't I jeopardize it with my inexperience?

A. This question brings me back to my early days of long-distance backpacking and the intense frustration of hiking with a much more experienced and speedy partner.

But as they say, walk before you run. Or walk before you backpack.

Before you start packing your food drops for the nearly 2700-mile-long PCT, you and your partner need to go on a hike together. You also need to start talking. Have a conversation about what you'll do if the trail proves too hard, if it's not what you expected, if you can't handle the mileage, or if you find out that you just plain hate the idea of walking 650 miles through rattlesnake country.

Because, yes—I'm not going to sugarcoat it—the PCT boasts rattlesnakes, steep slippery ice slopes, and raging creeks to cross (no tightropes, though), as well as 100-degree temperatures, freezing nights, days of rain, and hordes of mosquitoes. But it also offers plenty of payback: pristine lakes, gorgeous views, night skies shimmering with starshine, and some of the most beautiful country to be found anywhere. For me, the PCT was a lifetime highlight. But it was very hard. And I *like* this stuff!

The key question: Is this something *you* want to do? You're a good sport to go along with your boyfriend's dream, but is this your dream, too? The fact is, you can't walk 2700 miles on someone else's motivation. I'm not so much worried about your jeopardizing his trip, but you may be putting your relationship on the line. As an experienced hiker, your boyfriend undoubtedly has ideas about what the trip will be like. He might be expecting you to grow into them or fall in line with them. What if you can't handle the mileage? What if you freak out in the snow? Will he be willing to slow down? Change his plans? Support your decision to leave the trail? If so, you have a chance. If not, you're in for trouble.

The bottom line: Sure, inexperienced people can hike long trails—they do it every year. Anyone who is reasonably fit and in good health can do the PCT. But it's not easy. And those who succeed are following their dream, not someone else's.

Basics of a Personal Nature.

Q. What does a woman do when she gets her "monthly friend" on the trip? I need a woman's answer. What about disposal, coping, privacy, cleaning up?

A. Thanks for asking a question a *lot* of other women are wondering about—whether they're going for a day hike or a thru-hike.

First, I'm going to recommend a terrific book: *Women and Thru-Hiking on the Appalachian Trail* by Beverly Hugo, which discusses the issue in detail, as well as just about anything else a female hiker would want to know, no matter where she is hiking.

But let me cover some of the basics here:

Getting your period on a hike is a slight inconvenience, nothing more. (And note that on long hikes, many women actually skip periods or find that the flow lessens quite a bit.) Experiment to see which kinds of tampons you're most comfortable using when you're stuck somewhere without a toilet. Those with applicators make for more trash to pack out, but they may be more convenient to use. In addition to tampons, I always carry ultralight pads. That way, if I happen to be on a trail with a lot of other hikers and not a lot of trees and bushes to hide behind, I don't have to worry about accidents. This is especially true in bad weather, because you might not want to stop during a downpour. Using pads instead of or in addition to tampons gives you freedom to pick and choose when to take care of yourself. Keep some TP in a pocket, and during "that time of the month" keep your supplies in a place where you can get to them easily.

For cleanup, I carry a little extra water and a bandanna reserved for "personal" use. I also carry a bunch of small zipper-lock bags for the daily trash, and a larger bag in which to carry the small bags together. You'll find more opportunities to dispose of trash on the AT than you will on other trails. Sometimes, there are trash receptacles at road crossings and trailheads. If you can't find a place to dispose of sanitary products, you'll need to pack them out with your other garbage.

While it's not acceptable to bury the trash (animals will just dig it up), you may be able to burn it, assuming you are hiking where fires are permitted. I wouldn't recommend this for people hiking in the fragile desert and alpine areas of the West, but in temperate forests you can make fires in good conscience. If you can't burn your personal trash, you'll need to store it somewhere where animals won't be able to get at it, about 100 yards from your campsite. Hanging garbage in a bag from a tree branch is usually fine.

Menstruation and Grizzly Bears.

Q. Is it true that having your period increases the risk of bear attacks?

A. No. Studies have found no correlation between menstruation and bear attacks.

For peace of mind, you may want to burn your personal trash (see above); otherwise, hang it from a tree with your other garbage.

Gear That Fits.

Q. Is there any place I can go to find gear that is actually designed for women? This unisex business is for the birds.

A. You're right, not all unisex sizes work for women, especially those of us who have a few curves.

With some gear (tents and stoves, for example) gender is not an issue. But women can run into trouble if they try to use raingear, backpacks, sleeping bags, or boots designed for men.

With rain jackets, the arms of a man's jacket may be too long, and the cut around the hips too narrow. With rain pants, the seat and the distance from crotch to waist may be too small.

Unisex sleeping bags are often too long for women, and too narrow in the hips. Bags that are too long feel colder because there's extra space that needs to be warmed. Bags that are too narrow are uncomfortable and can also feel colder if the down fill is compressed.

Unisex packs tend to be too wide in the shoulders and too narrow at the hips.

Unisex hiking shorts just plain fit wrong all over.

Backpacker's annual *Gear Guide* highlights companies that make gear sized for women. For outdoor clothing, try the mail-order company Title Nine Sports, *(www.Title9Sports.com)*.

Chapter 8

Groups and Impact
LEADING OTHERS
AND TREADING LIGHTLY

I t's only natural to want to share the things we love with the people we love. That's certainly true with hiking.

Some of us share our love of the outdoors with family and friends. Others go a step further and lead groups—whether as volunteers for clubs, schools, churches, and organizations, or as professional outdoor teachers and guides.

Whether you're guiding your own family group or leading an organized expedition, your responsibility is the same: To ensure that everyone has a safe, enjoyable trip, and to minimize impacts on the backcountry and others on the trail. More may be merrier, but remember that the more people you have in your party, the greater impact you will have on trails, campsites, wildlife, and other hikers. Follow Leave-No-Trace guidelines, tread lightly, and be considerate—not just with waste disposal and cleanup, but with noise, especially if your group includes one or more high-impact noisemakers like dogs (see "Hiking with Rover," Chapter 2), small children, and cell phones (see below).

Becoming a Guide.

Q. I'd like to pursue a career in the outdoors. How do I become a hiking guide?

A. There are dozens of ways to work in the outdoors, from teaching in an outdoor education center to leading adventurous trips in exotic parts of the world.

No matter what kind of outdoor guide you become, you must have rock-solid skills in everything from backcountry cuisine to gear repair to emergency management. Equally important are your people skills. Are you level-headed? Even-tempered? Do you freak out in an emergency or handle things calmly? Do people listen to you?

Employers may require you to already have some experience. Perhaps you've been a park ranger or an outdoor education instructor; perhaps your wilderness "résumé" includes some trail-maintaining time. A good way to get in-field experience is by volunteering for one of the many nonprofit organizations that offer trips for members. Most have a process for training and selecting leaders. In the Sierra Club's Inner City Outings Program, for instance, you start as an assistant leader and move up when you've demonstrated your competence. You must also have a current first-aid certificate.

You can take classes in wilderness skills, first aid, and leadership. Some colleges offer programs in recreation with courses in wilderness leadership skills. One of the most prestigious outdoor schools for guides is the National Outdoor Leadership School. Their highly selective instructors' courses focus on minimum impact and backcountry skills. Outward Bound also offers a variety of outdoor programs, as do some retailers such as REI and EMS. Some guide services and wilderness schools train their own staff from scratch, so if you have your heart set on working for a particular company, ask first!

Leading groups is a big responsibility. While it sounds like fun, your real job is to make sure everyone *else* has fun. Days are long, and the pay can be shockingly low. The upside is that you get to do what you love, share your skills and knowledge with others, and maybe even travel to some of the world's most scenic places. More good news: There's a lot of turnover in this field, so openings are often available.

Are Low-impact Groups an Oxymoron?

Q. I'd like to lead groups for a local inner-city outings program because I think the best way to get people to care about the outdoors is to let them experience it themselves. But large groups bother me when I encounter them. Are there any strategies for low-impact leadership?

A. Indeed there are.

The first, and perhaps the most important thing you can do is keep the size of your group down! The maximum size should be no more than ten people (two leaders and eight participants), and fewer if regulations require

Large groups have an enormous impact on small shelters. Instead, camp out-of-sight in less-used areas and leave no trace.

it. If you have a larger group, split it up—and no, this doesn't mean walking a half mile apart and camping within hollering distance of each other!

Practice minimum-impact camping techniques (see accompanying Leave-No-Trace guidelines). Stay 200 feet away from water wherever possible. Bury solid waste in cat holes (again, away from water). Do not wash dishes or otherwise use soap directly in a lake or stream. Pack out whatever you pack in—including food garbage.

You can also minimize your impact by your choice of a trail or a campsite. Choose less-frequented trails where you'll encounter fewer people. The same goes for campsites. If you are hiking on a trail with a shelter system, be aware that your group will probably monopolize the entire shelter. If you really want to minimize your impact, camp somewhere else.

Cell Phones.

Q. When I go into the wilderness, I want to get away from civilization, and the last thing I want to hear is some bozo talking on the phone. What is proper backcountry etiquette with regard to cell phones?

A. I don't know that this issue has made it into Miss Manners's books yet (I haven't personally seen her on the trail, but maybe she's going incognito). You're certainly not alone in feeling that those ubiquitous noisy machines and the even noisier people who sometimes use them compromise our sense of wilderness. Not to mention the cell phone towers popping up on every high point. But you may as well tilt at windmills: Cell phones are in the woods to stay. Sometimes, as in the case of emergencies, they are even useful.

That said, readers who use cell phones should exercise some common courtesy. Not everyone wants to hear your call to your broker or babysitter, so keep your voice low, use the phone out of sight (and earshot) of others, and, unless you absolutely need it to be on, keep the ringer off while you are with other hikers. Some hikers cherish the sense of *not* being able to call friends, loved ones, and business associates. When you talk on a cell phone, you're bringing the "real" world into the wilderness—and some of us desperately want to escape the real world. Please be discreet.

Kid-Friendly Hikes.

Q. I love the outdoors, and I want my kids to love it, too. I'm taking them on their first backpacking trip. How do I make it special?

A. Focus on the things you love: identifying flowers and birds, picking berries, swimming in a creek, savoring a view. Point out the things you notice. You don't have to convince kids to enjoy the outdoors—there's just too much interesting stuff out there.

A few things to remember:

▲ Be sure kids have adequate gear that will keep them warm and dry. "Kid gear" may be little, but it has to do the same job that your gear does.
▲ Help kids monitor their feet so they don't get blisters. (See "Still Hobbling" in Chapter 9 for tips on avoiding blisters.)
▲ Plan a trip with an interesting and rewarding destination: a waterfall, a great view, a swimming hole.
▲ Keep the mileage conservative, and set an easy pace.
▲ Carry snacks, and plan kid-friendly meals (see "Feeding the Hungry Hordes," Chapter 3).

Mileage for Kids.

Q. I'm trying to plan a 3-day, 2-night hike for a group of 11-year-olds. How many miles a day can they do?

A. Is this the group of kids that plays basketball after school, or the group that sits around playing video games? As with adults, kids' fitness varies tremendously.

Mileage also depends on terrain, so consider how difficult the trail is. Family hiking experts agree that on average trails, most children can handle their age in mileage, with a cap at about 10 miles. They may, however, need to "break in" with shorter days. Kids older than 10 can hike farther than 10 miles, but only if they are in above-average shape.

Leave-No-Trace Principle #1: Plan Ahead and Prepare

▲ Know the regulations and special concerns for the area you'll visit. Prepare for extreme weather, hazards, and emergencies.

▲ Schedule your trip to avoid times of high use.

▲ Visit in small groups.

▲ Split larger parties into groups of four to six. Repackage food to minimize waste.

▲ Use a map and compass to eliminate the use of marking paint, rock cairns, or flagging.

Cold Weather and Kids.

Q. I've recently become a father. My son is 9 months old and loves to "hike" with me. So far we have had warm weather, but it is quickly turning to winter. What are some of the main things I should be concerned about when we go outside in the cold?

A. Kids and winter go together like snowflakes and Santa Claus. By thinking about safety and comfort before you head out, you're helping to ensure that your son enjoys his introduction to the great white season!

Nice sentiment, bad idea. Children are fascinated by animals, but they need supervision. Gently explain that feeding wild animals can make them dependent on human food.

The same principles that work for adults work for kids. The difference is that very small children can't tell you when they are starting to get cold. Also, if you're carrying your child, you may be working up quite a sweat while they sit there shivering. A few tips:

▲ Use synthetic garments like fleece and pile, not cotton.

▲ Dress your child in layers so you can adjust the temperature as needed.

▲ Be sure your child wears a hat, neck protection (a scarf or hood), and gloves.

▲ Your child will also need foul-weather protection, an outer layer of water-proof material.

▲ Take a bundle of extra clothes for a child who rides in a baby carrier.

▲ Start with short walks close to home to see how your child deals with the cold.

▲ Bring along a thermos of hot drinks and a couple of those chemical hand-warmers, just in case.

▲ On sunny days when you're hiking on snow, your child's eyes need protection, just like yours. Make sure he or she is wearing a pair of baby sunglasses and/or a hat with a visor.

▲ Take a change of diapers. A cold, wet diaper can contribute to hypothermia.

▲ Monitor your baby's condition. Don't hesitate to stop the hike if he or she seems cold or cranky, or if the weather is turning bad.

Crossing Creeks with Kids.

Q. I am taking two children on their first wilderness hike. We have to cross two thigh-deep creeks to get to our campsite. What is the best way to do this without staying wet half of the day?

A. Creek crossings can be tough, especially in late fall and early spring when the water can be stingingly cold. The other dilemma is gauging the flow of the current, and whether it is safe to cross. There's a big difference between a slow, lazy creek and a fast-flowing torrent. Fast-running high water can be tricky even for a full-grown adult. Remember, what is thigh deep for you might be chest deep for your kids. Be realistic when you gauge the difficulty of the crossing. Check it yourself before you start crossing with the kids. If conditions aren't what you expected, be willing to turn back.

If you think that your kids can make it, you should cross together as a group, holding hands, the smallest person in the middle and the biggest (and strongest) upstream to help break the current. Make sure everyone is wearing some kind of footwear.

It's a drag to walk in wet boots; crossing water in a pair of sports sandals is a good solution. Make sure the sandals are fastened securely. If you're not carrying sports sandals, take off your boots, remove socks and insoles, then put the boots back on and lace them tightly around your bare feet. After you walk across, you'll have dry socks and insoles, and the boots won't feel so wet.

Piggybacking is not as good a solution as it may seem unless the kids are small enough to carry easily (but big enough to hang on tight) and the creek is slow. You'll have to make several crossings. Remember to face into the current; it's easier to keep your balance when you meet the force of the water head-on. Trekking poles also help, although a strong current can create drag and pull them downstream from you. How helpful they are will depend on the current, the water depth, and how skilled you are at using them.

I don't advise using a rope, unless you are trained in river rescue. Ropes can entangle and drown people. The force of moving water on a rope is unbelievably strong. If you think you need a rope, you probably need to plan a different hike! However, a fixed rope already installed across a river can be used as a balance aid, holding onto it from the *downstream* side. *Never* clip in to a fixed rope with a carabiner when crossing a river; if you lost your balance, you could be held under and drowned.

If the river is running high due to spring and summer snowmelt, you should try (if possible) to cross in the morning, when it may be running slower. Pay attention to the cold: Cold water plus cold air is a recipe for hypothermia. Bring extra clothes, and

> ## Leave-No-Trace Principle #2: Travel and Camp on Durable Surfaces
>
> ▲ Durable surfaces include established trails and campsites, rock, gravel, dry grasses, or snow.
> ▲ Protect riparian areas by camping at least 200 feet from lakes and streams.
> ▲ Good campsites are found, not made. Altering a site is not necessary.
> ▲ In popular areas:
>   Concentrate use on existing trails and campsites.
>   Walk single file in the middle of the trail, even when wet or muddy.
>   Keep campsites small. Focus activity in areas where vegetation is absent.
> ▲ In pristine areas:
>   Disperse use to prevent the creation of campsites and trails.
>   Avoid places where impacts are just beginning.

> ## Leave-No-Trace Principle #3: Dispose of Waste Properly
>
> ▲ Pack it in, pack it out. Inspect your campsite and rest areas for trash or spilled foods. Pack out all trash, leftover food, and litter.
> ▲ Deposit solid human waste in cat holes dug 6 to 8 inches deep at least 200 feet from water, camp, and trails. Cover and disguise the cat hole when finished.
> ▲ Pack out toilet paper and hygiene products.
> ▲ To wash yourself or your dishes, carry water 200 feet away from streams or lakes and use small amounts of biodegradable soap. Scatter strained dishwater.

have some "warmies" (hat, gloves, fleece jacket) handy so that if the kids chill after a crossing, they can put something on right away. Hot drinks are another good idea.

Finally, talk to rangers to get a feel for current conditions, and maybe even alternatives. Don't be afraid to bail out if the creek is running too high. After all, the whole point of a family outing is to have fun, not a hair-raising adventure.

Leader Responsibility.

Q. I lead trips for a seniors' hiking club. One of our members has been handicapped due to a stroke. She demands to go on hikes, but she falls repeatedly. She needs help getting up; she also needs assistance traversing some of the terrain. But she refuses to wear hiking boots or to use a walking stick. She and her companion slow down everything and are very demanding. She says she will sue if she can't go on hikes. Her behavior is causing others to not go. Any suggestions?

A. When I led trips for a local Sierra Club chapter, the official policy was that leaders were responsible for interviewing prospective hikers to be sure they could handle the demands of the outing. I discussed this issue with one of the leaders of the New York–North Jersey Chapter of the Appalachian Hiking Club (which runs hundreds of trips a year). He said, "AMC leaders have absolute discretion—and indeed the responsibility—to be sure that people can handle the trip they want to go on, both mentally and physically. Otherwise, a trip can be a disaster. It's not a question of handicapped access. It's a question of whether the trip can exist."

You should also consider that if this is the type of person to wave the threat of a lawsuit around, what would stop her from suing the club if she were injured on one of these hikes? Her disabilities could cause injuries to others. What if she falls and knocks someone else over? What if she subjects herself and others to hypothermia when rain makes the trail slippery and she can't make it back to the trailhead? They could sue, too. What a mess.

I don't think that any reasonable person would begrudge a handicapped person's right to participate in outdoor activities. Your outings committee should certainly try to provide trips suitable for the ability levels of all its members. You might find that others in your community would welcome the opportunity to participate in outdoor activities.

But it is absolutely appropriate to limit participation in any particular hike to people who have the fitness, skills, and physical ability to handle its demands. It is also appropriate to require the use of equipment like hiking boots and trekking poles.

In inclement weather, hiking with a group offers a margin of safety in case someone becomes hypothermic or disoriented in the fog.

Keeping a Group Together.

Q. I'm leading a physically mismatched group of kids. The last time we hiked, we were strung out over a mile and one of the kids took a wrong turn. How can I keep the group together?

A. If you have two leaders, you could divide the group into faster and slower groups. Another strategy is to have a lead hiker and a "sweep." The lead hiker stops at every intersection to wait for everyone else. Waiting time can be used as time for snack breaks or games. The "sweep" stays behind (or with) the slowest hiker. This way, everyone is free to walk at his or her own pace.

If a slower hiker is really having a hard time, you might consider having one of the leaders (or even one of the stronger kids) take on a little extra pack weight. Nothing evens out a group's pace as quickly as a weight redistribution!

> **Leave-No-Trace Principle #7:**
> **Be Considerate of Other Visitors**
>
> ▲ Respect other visitors and protect the quality of their experience.
> ▲ Be courteous. Yield to other users on the trail.
> ▲ Step to the downhill side of the trail when encountering pack stock.
> ▲ Take breaks and camp away from trails and other visitors.
> ▲ Let nature's sounds prevail. Avoid loud voices and noises.

Chapter 9

Health, Fitness, and Safety
PREPARING—AND REPAIRING—
YOUR BODY

Backcountry safety is another subject that could take up an entire book, and indeed, *Wilderness 911*, by Eric Weiss, in this series of Backpacker/ Mountaineers Books titles, addresses the issue in detail. But questions pop up, anyway—usually because in our wonderfully unpredictable world, things don't always go as planned, and there are exceptions to every rule. The following questions address some of these situations. In addition, personal safety and security precautions for women are covered in Chapter 7, and personal safety in dealing with wild animals is covered in Chapter 10.

Mountain-Ready

Mountain Self-rescue.

Q. If you were hiking or skiing in the mountains and you had an accident, how would you get off the mountain?

A. This is precisely why one of the first rules of safe backcountry travel is— don't go alone.

If you have a hiking partner, he or she can help make you comfortable and go for help. If your injuries aren't too serious, hiking partners can help you by taking some of your gear, or by assisting you as you walk out.

Some equipment can help you out of a tight spot: A GPS unit (see Chapter 5) identifies your location precisely. If your hiking partner (or a kind stranger happening to pass by) walks out to get help, he or she will be able to tell rescuers where you are. New on the market is a combination cell phone GPS unit. Assuming you're in range of a cellular communications tower, this gizmo allows you to call for help and tell rescuers your precise location.

If you have neither a partner nor a cell phone and you can't walk out, you just might have to wait until someone—a rescuer or another hiker—finds you. Treat yourself for shock by keeping warm, drinking fluids, and elevating your feet. Put yourself in a position (like right in the middle of a trail) where you'll be obvious if anyone comes by, even if you're asleep. You can use smoky fires, a signal mirror, a whistle, or arrangements of bright-colored clothing to call attention to your position. Make sure that you are out in the open so you can be seen.

Lightning Above Tree line.

Q. I know you're supposed to descend from exposed ridges when there's thunder and lightning, but sometimes that's not possible above tree line. What should you do to keep safe when there's nowhere to hide?

A. Many mountain storms come in during the afternoon, so my first piece of advice is hike high early in the day, whenever possible.

But sometimes nature isn't predictable. And some trails stay high for many miles at a time, making it impossible to avoid the high country in the afternoon.

Staying safe during a lightning storm is somewhat counterintuitive. Lightning strikes from the sky, but you can also be hit by so-called ground lightning. You might think of taking shelter in a cave, but shallow caves and overhangs actually attract lightning as it courses along the ground. So do lone trees; so do standing pools of water.

The best thing you can do is lose some altitude. Even a little bit helps. On

It's counterintuitive, but this overhanging rock would be a terrible place to take shelter under during an electrical storm. It actually attracts lightning.

the summit of Mount Thielsen in Oregon, there is a glassy substance called fulgarite, which is created by repeated lightning strikes. The substance is only found at the top of the mountain, indicating that lightning does indeed seek the high point. On Thielsen, as with other summits and ridges, if you descend just a little bit you significantly reduce the chance of being struck.

If you find yourself thinking that the lightning bolts seem right overhead and personally directed at you, take a defensive position. Squat on the ground, on a camping mattress, if you are carrying one. (It's a hard position to maintain; the idea is to get as low as you can and to keep the contact between you and the ground minimal.) Put down anything metal you might be carrying (ice axes, hiking sticks, packs with metal frames).

People who are struck by lightning may appear to be dead, with no heartbeat or respiration. This is a terrifying thing to happen in the middle of a wilderness, but often the victim can be revived with CPR. All backcountry hikers and climbers should be competent in first aid and CPR (classes are offered by the Red Cross).

Off-season Training.

Q. What is the best way to train for hiking in the off-season?

A. What off-season?

Okay, so maybe you don't like sleeping in the snow. What's a sunbird to do?

Backpacking requires endurance, which means that your heart and lungs should be aerobically fit. Anything you do, from kick-boxing to swimming, that helps get your heart and lungs in shape will help you meet the challenges of backpacking, even if the trail you happen to be hiking goes up something called "Cardiac Hill."

The next concern is strengthening your legs: quads, hamstrings, and calves. Running is probably the most efficient regimen, but day hiking works, too, especially if you can find some challenging hills to climb. If you live in northern climes, try cross-country skiing, which works everything all at once. If you really don't want to face the cold, try a treadmill or a stair-climber. For strength, you can add on some weight-lifting exercises.

Peak Condition.

Q. We're planning to day hike out West this summer. What's the best way to prepare for hiking at high elevations? We live in Florida. We work out on a treadmill, elevating it to simulate going uphill. Is this enough?

A. Some hikers say that the only way to get ready to put on a pack and walk uphill is to put on a pack and walk uphill. There is some truth to this statement—after all, nothing is really going to prepare you for the rigors of all-day mountain backpacking except doing it. But pre-hike fitness training helps make those early break-in days pleasant, not miserable. Just about any sort of aerobic exercise—even swimming and step aerobics classes—will help.

When we talk about getting fit for mountain backpacking, we're really talking about four things:

▲ The actual uphill walking. The muscles you'll be using are the calves, quads, hamstrings, and buttocks, so anything you can do to work those will help.

▲ The lungs and heart. To increase your cardiovascular fitness, you need to breathe hard and sweat! The payoff is when you tackle that first 3000-foot elevation gain.

▲ Your feet. Walk 50 miles or so, even if it's on a treadmill or a flat city street, to be sure your boots fit. I know it's hard in Florida, but try to find some-place with a slope, even if it's only 50 feet high, to make sure your boots can handle ups and downs. On downhills, your toes shouldn't press against the front of the boot; going uphill, your heels shouldn't slide up more than ¼ inch or so.

▲ And finally, altitude. Even altitudes as low as 6000 or 7000 feet can make you huff and puff like a chain-smoking couch potato. If you're going as high as 10,000 or 12,000 feet (or more) there is real potential for moun-tain sickness. There's nothing you can do to acclimate if you live at sea level, unless you have a mountain range handily nearby. So you need to plan a few gentle break-in days at gradually increasing altitudes in order to let your body get used to the change. Using the drug Diamox (see below) may be an option for you to discuss with your doctor.

Does Diamox Work?

Q. Several times I've tried to climb to 12,000 feet and have gotten altitude sickness. I'm going to Africa and I want to climb Kilimanjaro. Should I get a prescription for Diamox?

A. People differ widely in their response to altitude. Getting altitude sickness at 12,000 is not unusual, especially if you live at a much lower elevation and didn't have time to acclimate. If you tried to run from sea level to the top of Mount Hood and you got sick, that simply makes you normal. How-ever, most people can adjust to elevations of 12,000 or even more. If you weren't able to acclimate to 12,000 feet after several days, you may have a greater-than-normal susceptibility to altitude sickness.

On any major peak, the most important thing you can do is acclimate slowly. Sometimes that's easier said than done. In the case of Kilimanjaro,

Kilimanjaro rises to more than 19,000 feet. Many climbers use the drug Diamox to ward off altitude sickness on Africa's highest peak.

you could acclimate by climbing a smaller mountain first (15,000-foot Mount Meru is nearby). Or you can arrange to take extra days for your climb. The standard tourist route is usually completed in 5 days, but most people going up and down that fast do suffer from the altitude.

If you don't have enough time to climb another peak first or to take a slower route, you should talk to your doctor about Diamox. The drug has some potentially serious effects and contraindications, so it isn't for everyone. Diamox must be taken before you start showing signs of altitude sickness, and you should continue using it until you come back down again.

Health and First Aid

Painful Knees.

Q. I love to hike, but my knees don't agree. How can I prevent (or treat) a painful knee when I hike?

A. Most problem knees respond well to prevention:

▲ Strengthen the leg muscles that support your knees. Before you hike, work hamstrings, quads, and calves with weight-bearing exercises. It's best to check in with a certified trainer who can help you choose exercises that don't put too much stress on the knee itself.

▲ Use two hiking sticks. Hiking sticks take hundreds of pounds of pressure off your knees during a hiking day. They transfer that weight to your arms, which otherwise would dangle lazily doing nothing at all. Spring-loaded shock-absorbing hiking sticks take yet more stress off the knees— the springs absorb some of the shock whenever you have to take a big step

Trekking poles are helpful on difficult terrain and in snow.

down. Using a pair of hiking sticks is especially helpful on long and steep
downhills.

▲ Bring a knee bandage. You can carry a lightweight Ace bandage, but heavy-
  duty knee braces give better support to an achy knee.

▲ Cut back on the mileage and stay away from steep downhills, if possible.

If you're still hurting:

- ▲ See your doctor. Some knee pain is caused by breakdown of cartilage, which can sometimes be treated by taking supplements (such as glucosamine and chondroitin) on a regular basis. Other causes of knee pain, such as arthritis, may be treated with medication. Structural problems may be helped by orthopedic surgery.
- ▲ Don't overdo it on the painkillers. Pain is your body's way of telling you that something is wrong. You need to listen.

Still Hobbling.

Q. I've broken in my boots. I don't carry too much weight, and I don't do big mileage. But I still get blisters. What am I doing wrong?

A. It sounds like you have the basics covered. Here are a few other things to try:

- ▲ Stop and treat hot spots the instant you feel them starting. The most innocuous little rub takes only seconds to turn into a full-blown blister. Treat it immediately to prevent the situation from deteriorating.
- ▲ Pre-treat your feet in places that you know are trouble spots. No matter

Stopping to wash, dry, and check your feet is one way to keep them blister-free.

how well the boot fits, I always get little calluses that sometimes turn into blisters in the same place. I put a small strip of athletic tape on the problem area before I even start hiking.

- ▲ Wear a layer of thin sweat-wicking polypro socks next to your skin. Wear outer socks that are thick enough to provide cushioning and padding.
- ▲ Use foot-beds (also called insoles, or inserts). Some boot inserts can keep your feet from sliding around in the boot, which lessens friction, and hence, blisters.
- ▲ Stop during your hike to air out your feet. Taking a break to wash your feet with cold water can really help. Changing your socks helps, too.
- ▲ You could try using baby powder or talcum powder, which helps control and absorb sweat (a cause of blisters).
- ▲ It is possible that despite your attention to fit, your boots and your feet aren't a perfect match. If the above strategies don't help, you might want to check out Phil Oren's boot-fitting techniques (see Chapter 4).

Popping Blisters.

Q. I've heard you're not supposed to pop blisters, but if I keep hiking they end up popping by themselves. What should I do?

A. In a sterile world, you should not pop a blister. But the backpacking world is anything but sterile. As you found out from undoubtedly painful experience, blisters pop on their own if you keep hiking. It's much better if you pierce them yourself because you can treat and bandage them properly. Use a sterile needle (dip it in alcohol, or hold it under a flame with tweezers), then cover the blister with antibiotic ointment and dress it with a blister treatment like 2nd Skin. Don't be surprised if the blister fills up again; you may have to pierce it a couple of times.

Chafing Skin.

Q. Whenever I start hiking in the summer, I get a painful rash on my thighs. What can I do about it?

A. Between the legs is a common place for chafing rashes. Usually, they occur because of some combination of rubbing (which can be a problem for heavier hikers) and heat. Wearing extra-long shorts or (in cooler weather) leggings can help prevent the problem. Bicycle-style shorts (without the internal padding) are another solution. If you don't like the look, wear them under a looser pair.

Some hikers use Vaseline, cornstarch, or talcum powder to prevent heat rashes. Hydrocortisone cream is an effective treatment.

Electrolyte Replacement Drinks: Yes or No?

Q. My wife and I disagree about hydration. She believes that water is critical to good health and hydration, while I believe that sports drinks, tea, and other beverages are just as good. Who is right?

A. Your question isn't merely the subject of marital debate, it's an issue that is hotly argued among hikers, doctors, nutritionists, trainers, and other experts.

The answer depends on the type and amount of exertion you're getting, the heat, and your own body.

In general, water is best. (Score one for your wife.) After all, humans and other land animals have evolved to thrive on water. However, during prolonged and strenuous activity in hot weather, you may sweat so much that your body's electrolyte balance is compromised. Electrolyte replacement drinks (sports drinks) help restore crucial chemicals like sugars and salts that are lost during heavy sweating. (Score one for you.)

Many years ago, when hiking in Tennessee in 100-degree temperatures and humidity to match, I found myself constantly thirsty. I drank plenty of water, but it didn't quench my thirst. I kept urinating and feeling thirsty. Finally, I ate a meal loaded with salt, and felt much better. Years later, I learned about hyponatremia from a nurse and a ranger in the Grand Canyon. Hyponatremia is a dangerous condition that can occur when strenuous exercise takes place in extreme heat and electrolytes are lost. It is more common among ultra-endurance athletes and high-mileage long-distance hikers than among casual day hikers. But it is possible for day hikers in extreme environments to work so hard and sweat so much that their electrolytes are completely depleted. Drinking water alone doesn't solve the problem. In fact, unless you also replenish the electrolytes, drinking too much water can make things worse.

Hyponatremia is a serious condition that can lead to kidney failure, coma, and death. It is an emergency and requires immediate medical attention.

To lower the risk of hyponatremia, be conservative about exercising in extremely hot weather and be sure to eat. Foods like GORP contain some of the electrolytes you need: for instance, banana chips and sesame seeds have potassium, salted nuts

What Goes in a First-Aid Kit?

▲ Names and phone numbers of emergency contacts
▲ Blister treatment
▲ Antibiotic ointment
▲ Painkillers
▲ Latex gloves
▲ Tweezers and scissors
▲ Ace bandage
▲ Gauze rolls and pads
▲ Band-aids and butterfly bandages
▲ In addition, you might want to add some of the following, depending on your destination and the length of your trip: rubbing alcohol, antihistamines, calamine lotion or hydrocortisone cream, poison ivy treatment, personal medications.

One of the best ways to maintain your trail-health is to take breaks and drink water often. Although if you take a break in the middle of the trail, be prepared to get up and move if you see another hiker coming your way.

have sodium, and raisins have sugar. Another field treatment for dehydration is to prepare a mixture of 1 liter of water with a couple of teaspoons of sugar and a pinch of salt. Sports drinks work on the same principle. Grand Canyon rangers, who have plenty of experience treating dehydration, keep sports drinks on hand to help rehydrate hikers. Most experts recommend that these be used in diluted strength.

One other thing: You mentioned tea. Caffeinated drinks (tea, coffee, some sodas) are diuretics, which means that they actually contribute to dehydration. So in hot temperatures, leave the java and chai at home!

So the answer: Both you and your wife are right. Would that all marital spats were solved that easily!

Do I *Really* Need to Filter Water?

Q. I've been drinking backcountry water for years. But every guidebook and every forest service map now tells me to filter every drop, even from high mountain streams. Is this necessary? Or is it hype?

A. As a general rule, yes, it's necessary to filter or otherwise treat backcountry water.

Not everybody does, of course. In some remote places, the water is still clean and safe. You will often see hikers drinking straight from streams. But they are taking a risk.

The problem is that it's impossible to tell which water is pure and which contains microbes and parasites that will wreak havoc with your health, not to mention your hike.

Places where you need to be especially careful: Anywhere near towns and villages. Anywhere near farms or livestock. Anywhere near large concentrations of wild animals. Any place where large numbers of people camp. Anywhere near old mines (because of metals or chemicals leaching into the soil). You should also avoid springs in very boggy or soggy ground (because animal feces can seep into the drinking water), and water sources downstream of beaver dams.

Always filter water from open sources like a lake or pond.

What's left? A few big, high, remote wildernesses. Ask locally. Rangers are usually instructed to tell you to filter your water. If you ask them what *they* actually do, you'll get a more accurate picture of the actual risk.

How Purifiers Work.

Q. I'm confused. If you use iodine tablets to purify water, you need to wait about 20 minutes for the iodine to work. But if you use purifiers, which have iodine filters, you can drink the water immediately. How is it that iodine tablets require 20 minutes to work, but purifiers work immediately?

A. Iodine tablets take a long time to work because the *Giardia* cysts are very tough, and it takes at least 20 minutes (longer in very cold water) for iodine to penetrate them. In purifiers, the filter element takes care of *Giardia* by straining it. The iodine is there not to kill *Giardia,* but to kill viruses, which are too small for filters to catch. Viruses are much less hardy than *Giardia* protozoa, so it only takes a few seconds of contact for iodine to kill them.

Third-World Water.

Q. Our family is planning a one-year adventure around the world. We will backpack and stay in cities. We are planning to filter our water, since iodine isn't safe for a whole year. But would filtering plus chlorine bleach or iodine be better? What would you do on such an extended trip?

A. Drinking clean water is indeed an important consideration both in the backcountry and when you're staying in cities in developing countries. (I've gotten far more ill in cities than I've ever gotten in the great outdoors.)

Filtering a year's worth of water would be a major chore, but using iodine for a year isn't such a good idea either, because sustained overuse can cause thyroid damage. Fortunately, in cities and even in small towns, bottled water is widely available and inexpensive. In the few remote villages where bottled water isn't available, you'll almost always be able to buy soft drinks. (It's disconcerting to realize that while you may be on the adventure of a lifetime, Coke and Pepsi have gotten there first!)

But you should have some means of purifying water as a backup. I alternate between iodine tablets (when I'm lazy) and a purifying filter, which uses both a filter (to remove larger cysts, bacteria, and protozoa) and a small amount of iodine (to kill viruses). Whatever system you use, be sure it eliminates all these types of organisms.

A couple of other hints for safe drinking water in less-developed countries:
▲ Avoid ice, which could be made from unsafe water.
▲ Use filtered or bottled water to brush your teeth.

- Be wary of utensils and plates. I've seen plates dipped into a bucket of gray-brown water, and then immediately used to serve food. Unfortunately, there's not much you can do about this. If you see something like this happening, ask to rinse and dry the plate yourself, or use your own plate and utensils.
- Open your own bottled drinks. Sometimes, locals politely want to present you with a clean bottle with no dust on it, so they wipe the bottle with dirty water before opening it.
- Talk to your doctor about carrying an all-purpose antibiotic—just in case.

Immune to Poison Ivy?

Q. I thought I was immune, but this winter I got a rash the doctor said was poison ivy. How can a non-allergic person get poison ivy in the winter?

A. The dermatitis you get as a result of contact with poison ivy, poison oak, or poison sumac is an allergic reaction to a substance called urushiol. Urushiol is found on all parts of the poison ivy, oak, and sumac plants, including the

Learn to recognize poison ivy in all stages of its life cycle. The three-leaved clusters are a tell tale sign that this is a plant to avoid. So are the "hairy" vines and the shape of the branches.

roots and bare branches in the winter. It is indeed possible to get poison ivy in the winter without even knowing that you've touched the plant, unless you can recognize and avoid the bare branches. (They have a distinctive look: thin forked branches that reach straight out, and then up a little.)

As for immunity, don't bet on it. As with other allergies, the more you are exposed to poison ivy, the more allergic you become to it. You may have indeed been "immune" in the past, but you've obviously developed a sensitivity.

Post-Ivy Defense.

Q. Is there any way to prevent an attack of poison ivy after you've walked through a patch?

A. There are several ways, but it depends how allergic you are and how thoroughly you immersed yourself in the stuff. First, wash the affected area with cold water before the rash has time to fully penetrate the skin (about 30 minutes after exposure). If you have rubbing alcohol available, use it (don't rub it in, just lightly rinse the skin). Other products useful for removing poison ivy resin include Technu Poison Oak-N-Ivy Cleaner and Dr. West's Ivy Detox Cleanser. Be sure to wash your hands (including under your fingernails) to prevent spreading the resin to other body parts. Wash your clothes, too, because the resin can stay active for a long time.

Lyme Disease.

Q. I live in Wisconsin and I'm planning to hike some of the Ice Age Trail this summer. I've heard horror stories about Lyme disease. How much of a problem is it?

A. Lyme disease was described for the first time about 25 years ago in Connecticut, but is now common throughout the United States, wherever deer ticks are found. It is most common in the Northeast, the upper Midwest, and along the Pacific Coast.

The disease can be treated by antibiotics, but it is often difficult to diagnose. The telltale red bull's-eye rash you may have read about only occurs in some cases. Other symptoms can include inflammation, aching joints, headaches, fever, and itching (and these, of course, are common symptoms for a wide range of ailments). If untreated, the disease can cause more serious muscular, neurological, or cardiac problems.

To help prevent contracting Lyme disease while hiking in tick country, wear light-colored long-sleeved shirts and long pants tucked into your socks. The ticks will be more visible on light clothing. Check your skin frequently for ticks (they can be as small as a pinhead), paying close attention to warm sweaty places like between your toes and around your waist. Use insect repellent. Also, talk to your doctor about an immunization. A vaccine against Lyme disease is available, although it is not 100 percent effective.

Snakebite.

Q. What should I do if I'm in the wilderness and get bitten by a venomous snake?

A. First things first: Don't panic!

According to the FDA, of about 8000 people who are bitten in the United States each year by venomous snakes, only nine to fifteen die, so the odds are certainly in your favor. The amount of toxic venom varies widely: In 20 to 30 percent of cases, no venom at all is injected. Nonetheless, a bite from a venomous snake (or any snake you can't identify) should be considered a medical emergency. You need to get to a hospital.

When you're backpacking, getting to a hospital may be a major expedition in itself. What you do will depend on how far away you are from a road, whether you have a cell phone and can call for help, and whether or not you can walk.

First aid includes washing the bite with soap and water, immobilizing the bitten area, and keeping it lower than the heart. Additionally, if a victim is unable to reach medical care within 30 minutes, the Red Cross recommends that a bandage can be wrapped 2 to 4 inches above the bite to help slow the spread of the venom. The bandage should be loose enough that a finger can slip beneath it so that it does not stop the flow of blood. A controversial measure recommended by some (but not all) experts is the use of a suction device, which is often included in commercial snakebite kits. The device is placed over the bite to help draw venom out without making a cut.

Medical professionals are nearly unanimous about what not to do:

- ▲ Do not use ice. Research has shown this to be potentially harmful.
- ▲ Do not use a tourniquet, which stops blood flow and could result in the loss of the limb.
- ▲ Do not cut an incision into the wound. Researchers agree that this once-popular method has not been proven useful. It can cause infection or can even cause the venom to spread.

Chapter 10

The Natural World
INTERACTING WITH YOUR ENVIRONMENT

Any writer tackling a chapter called "The Natural World" should admit defeat before she even begins. The subject deserves a library, not a chapter. But there are certain phenomena that seem to capture the attention of hikers. Some aspects of the natural world affect us directly, like the weather. Other phenomena, like the northern lights, meteor showers, or hawk migrations, simply overwhelm us with their drama and beauty. And then there is our inevitable fascination—and sometimes fear of—lions and tigers and bears, not to mention snakes, skunks, porcupines, and "killer grouse." Intrigued? Read on.

Weather and Sky

Weather Indicators.

Q. Short of carrying a short-wave radio with me, is there any way for me to predict the weather while on a hike?

A. Predicting the weather is not as easy as listening to a forecast, since the weather in the nearest city can be very different than the weather in your hiking destination (especially if you're headed into the mountains). So hikers sometimes try to make their own predictions, relying on—or, as the case may be, ignoring—dozens of folk signs that purport to foretell the weather. Many of these signs do have some scientific basis, revealing information about barometric pressure and colliding weather fronts.

Probably one of the most familiar weather signs is "Red sky in the morning, sailors take warning. Red sky at night, sailor's delight." Translation: Brilliant sunsets are good news; brilliant sunrises, bad news. Since weather systems generally move from west to east, clouds from a storm departing east at sunset are illuminated by the setting sun, whereas morning clouds from a storm approaching from the west are illuminated by the rising sun.

Other warning signs are cloud formations known as "mares' tails" and "mackerel scales." These high cirrus clouds look like wispy commas, or (perhaps) horses' tails. Usually, they foretell good weather for the rest of the day, but when they are followed by the solid, thicker cloud layer, which looks like the scales on a fish, it's a sign that bad weather is coming in 24 to 36 hours.

Puffy white cumulus clouds in a blue sky are a sign of immediate good weather; however, when they also start to gather and darken, they herald a thunderstorm.

Decreasing barometric pressure is another sign of bad weather. Understanding weather patterns is a complex art and science, but basically, a high-pressure system brings fair, dry weather, whereas a low-pressure system brings unsettled weather and moisture. When the atmospheric pressure (measured on a barometer) drops, the lower barometric reading indicates a low-pressure system is approaching. The rate of the change in pressure is also an indicator: When the pressure falls quickly, you can expect a more powerful storm than if the pressure drop is more gradual.

Even if you don't carry a barometer, you can tell if the pressure is changing by looking at an altimeter (if you carry one); altimeters work by measuring atmospheric (air) pressure and converting it into altitude. A change of 100 feet on the altimeter equals a difference of 0.10 on a barometer, an average barometric reading being 29.92. If, when you went to bed at night, the altimeter told you that you were camped at 600 feet, and in the morning it reads 500 feet, it's probably because the atmospheric pressure is changing for the better (a lower reading on the altimeter translates to higher air pressure and fairer weather).

If you set your altimeter to your known altitude (from a topo map) and you notice a change later in the day, it's a sign of a change in the air pressure. Remember to adjust for any change in altitude you made during the day's travel. If the altimeter says that you are lower than you are, the pressure has risen, and you can expect good weather. If it says you are higher up, the pressure has dropped, and poor weather could be on the way.

If you don't have an altimeter, there are other ways to tell what the

A sky full of trouble in the North Cascades: High cirrus formations like this ("mares' tales" and "mackerel scales") foretell bad weather.

barometer is doing. If smoke from a fire is rising straight up, indicating a stable air mass, you can expect good weather. If the smoke lingers close to the ground, especially after the morning sun is up, expect bad weather. The birds and bees also give warnings: Since lower pressure tends to dissipate scents that are close to the ground, insects will respond to lower air pressure by hovering close to the ground and moving in a straight line, and the birds will fly lower, in order to better follow their food source's scent.

Other signs of imminent unsettled weather include a halo around the moon (made by the same "mackerel sky" clouds), wind shifting to the east, rising temperatures at night, clouds moving in different directions at different levels, steadily rising wind speeds, and updrafts that make leaves tremble so their undersides show.

Clear weather is heralded by falling temperatures (especially in the afternoon), dry cold winds, wind shifting to the west, breaking clouds, dew or frost at night, dew on the ground in the morning, clear stars, and noisy frogs.

All of the above notwithstanding, there's only one thing you can really predict about the weather: It'll change! Pack accordingly.

Mountain Weather.

Q. Why is the weather forecast in the town I live in completely unreliable for the mountains only a few miles away?

A. Mountains make their own weather systems. These so-called orographic effects include decreasing temperature and increasing precipitation.

On average, every 1000-foot rise in elevation lowers the temperature by between 3 and 5½ degrees Fahrenheit. Thus, a 3000-foot climb (not unusual in mountainous terrain) can result in a loss of between 9 and 16½ degrees.

Altitude also affects precipitation. Clouds and moisture-bearing winds rise as they pass over mountain ranges. As they rise, the temperature decreases, causing moisture to condense and form rain. This phenomenon explains why the mountains of southern California and Arizona can be covered with snow, even though they are surrounded by desert.

You'll also find higher winds at altitude, especially on exposed slopes. The resulting wind chill can be severe.

Northern Lights.

Q. What exactly are the northern lights and where can I see them?

A. Northern lights begin with a full-fledged nuclear explosion. Solar explosions on the sun throw electrons and protons into space. When these particles reach the Earth's atmosphere, they are caught by its magnetic field, which pulls them either north or south to one of the poles. En route, the particles collide with gas molecules in our atmosphere. The energy released by the collision is seen as the northern lights (aurora borealis) or the southern lights (aurora australis).

The region from which these displays are visible varies. In November 2001, the northern lights were visible as far south as Texas—and once every 200 years, they can be seen from the equator! But if you're intent on seeing the northern lights, the most consistently reliable observation points include northern Scandinavia, all of Greenland and the Svalbard archipelago (in the Arctic Ocean), northern Alaska, northern Canada, and northern Russia. The northern lights are most frequently seen in early spring and late autumn between 10 P.M. and midnight.

Shooting Stars.

Q. What are shooting stars, and when is the best time to see them?

A. Meteor showers occur when small fragments of cosmic debris enter the Earth's atmosphere at extremely high speed. A comet's orbit is filled with large amounts of small particles—a sort of meteoroid "stream." When the Earth's roughly circular orbit intersects the elliptical orbit of a comet, it also intersects the meteoroid stream trailing behind. This intersection of orbits, which takes place for a few days at the same time each year, produces a meteor shower.

Meteor showers appear to come from a single point in the sky. The showers are named for the constellation they seem to be radiating from during their peak. The meteor shower most often seen by backpackers is the Perseid shower, which takes place in late July through mid-August, and apparently originates from the constellation Perseus.

For a schedule of the most common meteor showers, see *www.comets. amsmeteors.org.*

Mountain and Forest

What Determines Tree Line?

Q. Why is tree line so variable from place to place? In Oregon, it's around 6000 feet. In New Hampshire, it's less than 5000 feet. In Colorado, it's above 11,000 feet.

A. Tree line is the approximate line above which trees can't grow because the climate is too harsh. (Timberline, by contrast, is the line above which commercially viable forests don't grow. You may find trees above timberline, but you won't find loggers!)

Tree line (and timberline) varies according to the prevailing climate, which is affected by latitude and weather fronts. Oregon's tree line is lower than Washington's, which is lower than Alaska's.

Latitude isn't the only factor. For example, tree line in the White Mountains of New Hampshire is around 5000 feet. At the same latitude in Europe, tree line is around 7000 feet. This is because Europe is warmed by the Gulf Stream. To understand just how much difference this makes, consider that Madrid is approximately at the same latitude as New York; Milan is approximately the same latitude as north-central New Hampshire.

It's worth noting that Europe's Alps sometimes appear to be much more massive than our American mountains because so much of them lies above tree line. In Colorado, for instance, tree line is around 11,000 feet. Only

Tree line in southern Colorado is at about 11,000 feet.

2000 to 3000 feet of even the highest mountains are above the tree line. In the Alps, a 14,000-foot peak may have more than 7000 feet above the tree line, much of which is in the dramatic rock-and-ice zone.

Why are the Southern Balds Bald?

Q. If there are no mountains above tree line in the southern Appalachians (as I've read), why are there no trees on the southern Balds?

A. You're right. Using latitude as the basis for calculations, scientists say that tree line in the southern Appalachians should be above 7000 feet. The highest mountain on the East Coast is North Carolina's 6684-foot Mount Mitchell, so technically, there is no such thing as "above-tree line" in the southern Appalachians.

Nonetheless, some (but by no means all) of the higher peaks in the southern Appalachians have no trees. The reason remains an enduring mystery. Theories include the long-term effects of Indian use of fire for forest management and hunting, grazing, high winds, or some combination. In recent years, these peaks have started looking like they've been been taking a mountain's equivalent of Rogaine: They are no longer completely bald, but are covered with patches of rhododendron.

Forest Fire.

Q. Is it true that some forest fires are good for the forest? What should I do if I'm caught in one?

A. Smokey the Bear notwithstanding, forest fires are part of the natural cycle of certain kinds of forests, including the coniferous forests that cover so much of our Western mountains. Fire pops open the cones in some species, allowing them to germinate. It opens the canopy, allowing light in for new growth. And it spreads a layer of fertile ash over the soil. Without periodic small fires, the amount of dead flammable wood in a forest would grow until a lightning strike could set off a major conflagration that would threaten the entire forest and nearby communities.

As managers and scientists have come to better understand the role of fire in the ecosystem, they have begun to allow certain fires to burn. Fire management is a complex process. While managers take into account moisture levels, the amount of dead wood in a forest, the weather forecast, and the proximity to human communities, they cannot always predict the course a fire will take. Sometimes, fires that were supposedly "controlled" end up burning out of control.

Information about fire danger is available at ranger stations. During a controlled burn, land managers closely monitor the fires and post information at trailheads, including information about trail closures and alternate routes.

Wildfires rarely start as full-scale conflagrations, so you'll usually have plenty of time to move away from them. Unless a fire is truly out of control, it is unlikely to jump to the next drainage (fires will move in an uphill direction as they burn, but rarely will they jump over a ridge and start moving downhill). So if you need to get away from a fire, moving over to the next drainage should solve the problem.

The Federal Emergency Management Agency recommends the following steps if you are caught in a forest fire:

Do not try to outrun it! If possible, crouch in a river or pond. Cover your head and body with wet clothing. If there is no water nearby, look for shelter in a cleared area or on rocky, non-flammable ground. Lie flat and if possible, cover your body with soil. Breathe air close to the ground, if possible through a wet cloth, which will protect your lungs from being burned by the smoke.

In hiking long distances or between two points, you may have no choice but to pass through an area that has recently burned. Check with land managers before entering such an area: Hot spots can flare up without notice.

Wildlife Encounters

Seeing Animals.
Q. I like to photograph animals. When and where are the best times to see them?

A. Rangers at national parks and forests can often tell you when and where to see certain animals. In Maine's Baxter State Park, there's a marked "moose crossing" that delivers a reliable sighting. Shenandoah National Park's Skyline Drive meanders past meadows where deer seem always to be grazing. Same goes for elk in Rocky Mountain National Park during the fall rutting season.

If you don't have local knowledge to guide you, the following tips will help.

▲ Stay still and quiet. The more you blend into the environment, the more animals you'll see.

▲ Avoid wearing perfumed soaps. You *want* to smell like you've been in the woods for a week!

▲ Go near a water source, or follow a trail that looks as if it's frequently used by animals. (But don't perch directly at the water source, especially in dry terrain—you may frighten away thirsty animals.)

▲ Look in ecotones, which are the places where two habitats intersect (like a meadow and a forest).

▲ Look at dawn and dusk, which are the most active times of day for many animals—also the best times for photography because of the color and slant of the light (see Chapter 5, "Lugging Camera Gear").

Hawk Migrations.
Q. I've heard that there are places where thousands of hawks fly by during their migration. When and where are the best places to see them?

A. Annual raptor migrations—including hawks, vultures, kestrels, osprey, and other birds of prey—are indeed a force of nature. At Pennsylvania's Hawk Mountain, for instance, an average of more than 18,000 raptors are counted during each fall migration (October to December).

There are dozens of hawk watching sites in the United States, from

In national parks, deer will often pose for pictures. Stay still and quiet, and look for them just before dusk or after dawn.

California to Maryland, from Texas to Maine. Migrations take place along established avian flyways during the spring and the fall. Peninsulas and mountain ranges attract large concentrations of birds, partly because of prevailing wind currents. Some sites do spring counts, and some do fall counts, depending on local migration patterns. For a list of watch sites, check *www.virtualbirder. com/vbirder/onLoc/onLocDirs/HAWK/bg/Find.html.*

Killer Grouse?

Q. I've heard that grouse will actually attack hikers. Is this true?

A. When people think of wild animal attacks, they're usually thinking of bears and rattlesnakes, but the dowdy little grouse proves the point that there is no force in nature so terrible as a mother's fury.

Grouse nest on the ground. When they choose their nesting sites in early spring, there aren't many hikers tromping by. By the time summer comes, what used to be a quiet trail turns into (from a grouse's perspective) an interstate highway. With the chicks already born, it's too late to move into a better neighborhood. Mom and Dad are left to hurl "I told you so's" at each other—and themselves at interlopers.

If you see a grouse on a trail in late spring and early summer, it will likely be doing one of two things: faking a broken wing, or running down the trail, stopping every now and again to check to see if you are still following it. It's trying to lure you away. If you stop right then and listen, you'll probably hear the "peep, peep" of the chicks. But you may also raise Mama's ire: Stick around too long, or continue in the direction of the family homestead, and she'll valiantly take you on—all two pounds of her—with flapping wings and pecking beak. The best thing to do when you see a grouse exhibiting protective behavior is to give her a break and get out of the vicinity. It's hard enough to raise a family these days.

Snakes.

Q. According to the guidebooks, there are venomous snakes on all the Triple Crown Trails—and most other trails, too. How much of a problem is this? How likely am I to encounter one when hiking?

A. On the three Triple Crown Trails put together (about 7800 miles), I saw fewer than twenty venomous snakes. One was a copperhead, the rest were rattlesnakes. I figure that works out to one venomous snake for every 390 miles of hiking. Most were along California's PCT; some were on the AT in Virginia and Pennsylvania.

With the exception of Maine, all the other states I walked through also have populations of venomous snakes. But I didn't see them. Snakes are as little interested in making your acquaintance as you are in making theirs. They have a sensitive heat-seeking mechanism that allows them to sense your presence as you approach them, and most often, they will simply slither away.

During the middle of the day, snakes may be too somnolent to move. A stream of hikers marching past a resting snake will eventually raise his (or her) ire. If you hear that heart-stopping rattle, step away from the noise, keeping an eye peeled. Once you've discovered the snake's location, you can walk around it. If thick brush makes moving around the snake impossible, you can try to force it to move by throwing small stones at it. Go easy: The object is to irritate it—not kill it.

When in snake country, watch where you put your feet and hands as you walk and climb—especially when rock scrambling. Never put your hands where you can't see them. During the heat of day, snakes hang out in the shade, in crevices between rocks and under bushes. In the cooler evening hours, you may see them along a trail, basking in what's left of the sun. When camping, keep your tent zipper closed to keep critters out.

Can you see the snake? Rattlesnakes are supremely camouflaged. When you hear an angry one (like this fellow) step away from the sound, then look for its source.

As for avoiding snakes, the higher you go, the fewer there are. Snakes are not often seen above tree line; their primary habitat is lower and warmer.

In the event of being bitten by a venomous snake, you will need to administer first aid and get to a hospital; see Chapter 9.

Deer and Salt.

Q. In three different national parks I've visited, rangers have warned me about deer doing damage in campsites. Since when is Bambi a hazard to hikers?

A. Your basic wild deer is no more a hazard to hikers than a dogwood tree. But in national parks, special circumstances exist. Wildlife enjoys complete protection—there's no hunting, even when animal populations become unsustainably large—so animals lose their natural fear of humans. Plus, with the high frequency of encounters between humans and animals, the animals learn to savor freeze-dried food.

In the case of deer, it's usually an issue of salt. Some environments, like Glacier National Park, don't have much natural salt, so the deer have learned to find it on sweaty T-shirts and smelly boots. People also often ignorantly lure deer into camp with treats like cereal bars. Guess what Bambi is looking for the next time someone sets up camp?

Giving wild animals human food is a bad idea all around. Although deer can be surprisingly tame, they can also be surprisingly aggressive and can seriously injure people who get too close. Sadly, in some parks, rangers have actually had to shoot starving deer that became too dependent on human food.

Storing Food.

Q. On a recent hike, I was harassed by animals all night. How should I store my food?

A. There are two animal issues on trails: Bears, and other critters. For information on bears and food precautions, see below.

It's far more common for mice and other small animals like raccoons, weasels, chipmunks, and skunks to visit your campsite in search of food. To foil them, keep your food together in a stuff sack and hang it from a tree branch or line between two trees. In a shelter, hang your food bag from a nail away from the wall so animals can't climb down to your food. Better yet, hang the food bags from one of the anti-mouse contraptions you'll often see in the lean-tos. These are made of string, a can, and a stick. Mice can't climb down over the can, so your food hangs safely undisturbed. Be sure to take all your food out of your pack, leave the zippers open (so critters don't chew their way in), and hang the pack from a nail, too.

When tenting, I usually hang food bags from tree branches to keep them off the ground and away from small animals. Another strategy is to camp off the beaten track, in more remote sites where animals are less likely to have developed thieving habits.

Skunks.

Q. During my last camping trip, two skunks came right into our campsite. We spent the whole night paralyzed with fear! What should we have done?

A. Other than avoiding populated campsites and keeping a clean camp, there's probably not much you can do to stop wildlife from visiting. Skunks are like any other critters. They visit in hopes of a free meal. And like other animals, they can be scared off. Unfortunately, they have a powerful defensive weapon, which may make you think twice about how aggressively you try to chase them away. If they persist in hanging around, your only choice is to quietly coexist or move.

Note also that wild animals, especially skunks and raccoons that seem excessively tame, act nervously aggressive, or (if nocturnal) are out in the middle of the day, may be rabid and should be avoided. A bite from a rabid animal is potentially fatal and requires immediate medical attention.

Skunks are members of the weasel family. They are not aggressive. Given a choice, a skunk would rather run away, but it will spray if it feels cornered. It's hard to miss the signs that a skunk is feeling upset: It will fluff its fur, shake its tail, stamp the ground with its forefeet, and growl. It may even stand up and spit! If all that doesn't convince you to back off, the skunk will, as a last resort, lift up its tail and spray.

Skunk spray may be one of the most unpleasant smells you'll ever encounter, in the wilderness or otherwise. It's not dangerous, although it can severely irritate your eyes and even cause temporary blindness. Washing with cold water will ease the irritation. The scent lingers on skin, clothes, and hair (not to mention pet fur) seemingly forever. You can wash your skin with carbolic soap, tomato juice, or vinegar. The same remedy goes for your pet. (Some commercial remedies are also available at pet stores.) According to the California Center for Wildlife, a remedy for skunk smells is to wash your pet with a mixture of one quart of three-percent peroxide, ¼ cup of baking soda, and 1 tablespoon of liquid hand soap. Clothes are usually a lost cause.

A Prickle of Porcupines?

Q. I hike with my dog and I'm worried about porcupines. Can they really throw their quills? Do they attack dogs?

A. Of the twenty-four species of porcupine, which inhabit North and South America, Africa, Asia, and Europe, nary a one can throw quills, despite popular superstition. And porcupines are certainly not predatory. Indeed, this slow-moving nocturnal rodent likes nothing more than to spend its days lazing in trees and rotted-out stumps. The spines are strictly a defensive weapon. When provoked, the porcupine slaps its tail against the head of a predator that gets too close. The quills—a typical porcupine may have 30,000 of them—are only loosely attached to the porcupine's skin, and can come out very quickly, which has led to the erroneous belief that porcupines attack by throwing quills.

Since people rarely feel the need to go nose-to-nose with a porcupine, they rarely have problems. Dogs are a different story. Dogs seem to view porcupines as potential playmates, or at least, as something worth exploring. Porcupines disagree. Your dog will lose this argument! The barbed quills are difficult to remove and can cause serious injury, infection, even death. Quills may break off at the skin level; the part that remains in the dog's body can migrate, damaging internal organs. You may be able to remove the quills yourself with pliers, but a dog that has suffered the losing end of an encounter with a porcupine should be taken to a vet; the injuries can be life-threatening.

Sometimes, porcupines visit campsites in search of salt, which they crave.

If you are staying in a trail shelter where porcupines are known to nose around, you should make sure your boots (which have sweat-soaked linings) and your pack (which has a sweat-soaked hipbelt) are safely stored; hang them from a hook in a shelter.

Oh, and yes, a group of porcupines really is called a prickle!

Dogs in Bear Country.

Q. I'm planning a trip into grizzly country with some friends. We are thinking of bringing a dog with us (we normally do). I know the debates about pooches in the backcountry. My question: Will we be increasing our risks of a bear encounter if we take Fido?

A. He's not really named Fido, is he?

Backcountry rangers at Yellowstone and Glacier National Parks say yes, you are increasing your risk of a bear encounter by bringing a dog. The theory is that dogs chase interesting scents, and when they find themselves overmatched by a bear, they'll run back to you—and possibly bring the bear with them. Even if you have the dog on a leash, its behavior during a bear encounter could be unpredictable. It might start barking, which could raise the hackles of a mama bear protecting her cubs. Or it could bust loose, leading to a free-for-all. A chance encounter with a griz is terrifying enough, without Fido barking up a storm.

A friend of mine is an avid hiker who walks with the help of a seeing-eye dog. Seeing-eye dogs, of course, are exempt from no-dog rules. Nonetheless, after talking with rangers in Glacier and Yellowstone about the potential risks, she decided not to hike in the backcountry with her extremely well trained, obedient, trail-savvy, leashed, and harnessed dog. If I were you, I'd follow her lead.

Bear Bags.

Q. I've always hung my food in trees, but recently I was told I wasn't doing it right. Is there a right way to hang your food?

A. Technically, yes, the counterbalance method is "the right way" to hang food in trees, along with other objects with smells that could attract animals— soap, toothpaste, cook pots, and garbage.

Here's how the counterbalance works: You throw a rope over a branch. The branch should be sturdy enough to hold the food but not sturdy enough to support the weight of a bear, and bags must be hung high enough that bears can't reach them.

Attach a food bag, and pull it up into the tree. Now, attach a counter-

The counterbalance method of bear bagging is the most effective way to foil an uninvited dinner guest.

balance (usually another food bag) to the other end of the rope. Tie off any extra rope, and push the second bag up with a hiking stick. To get the bags down in the morning, you just reach up and give one of the bags a push with the stick; gravity will do the rest.

Usually it doesn't much matter if your bear bags are perfectly hung. Your basic bear doesn't go sniffing around with its nose in the air waiting for food to fall from the sky. But in places like the High Sierra (including Yosemite, Kings Canyon, and Sequoia National Parks), Shenandoah National Park, and Great Smoky Mountains National Park, bears have learned to associate humans with food. Some bruins do indeed look treeward for food, and have developed amazingly effective strategies for knocking food bags out of trees, even when the bags are correctly hung.

Check the regulations and recommendations where you plan to hike. In many hiking areas, rangers recommend the counterbalance method. But some parks with serious bear problems are now requiring the use of installed food storage bins or bear-proof storage canisters.

Bear Canisters.

Q. Where I live in Virginia, we have black bears, but we just hang our food storage bags from trees. I am heading out to Washington. Should I invest in a bear-proof food canister?

A. On the face of it, I'd say no, unless you know you are going into an area that has severe animal problems. (Certain well-used campsites in the Olympic Mountains have recently had problems with raccoons, for example, necessitating new and stricter food storage regulations.) Before you go, check the current rules and recommendations by calling the national forest or park where you'll be hiking.

In general, however, black bears in Washington tend to be like black bears anywhere else—intelligent, adaptable, hungry, and clever, but not tame. Wild bears avoid people, although in popular camping areas they occasionally show up in hope of scoring a free meal. Using the counterbalance method of bear-bagging (see above) is usually sufficient.

Canisters are heavy and expensive, and they can hold only a limited amount of food. Another alternative worth a look is a new product called the UrSack, a lightweight stuff-sack made out of aramid fabric—the stuff they use to make bulletproof vests.

Grizzlies and Black Bears.

Q. I'm going to be hiking in Montana. How can I tell if I'm looking at a grizzly bear or a black bear?

A. If you look at photographs of grizzlies and black bears side-by-side, the differences are easy to see. Grizzlies (a subspecies of the brown bear) are much bigger than black bears. They have a dish-shaped face, whereas black bears have a "Roman" profile. And the grizzly's fur is indeed grizzled looking, with a silvery sheen to it. Despite the names, color isn't a reliable indicator of species—both bears can range in color from light cinnamons to deep browns.

In the wild, the differences may not be obvious, especially if all you see is the back of a bear as it disappears into the undergrowth. Even if you get a clear look, a juvenile grizzly may look like a black bear to you.

In the United States, the only states that have grizzly bears are Montana, Alaska, small parts of Wyoming and Idaho, and possibly Washington (where grizzly sightings are only rarely reported). Otherwise, if you see a bear, it's a black bear.

Black Bears.

Q. I'm going to be hiking in an area known to have a lot of black bears. How dangerous are they? What should I do if I see one?

A. Black bears are not usually dangerous to humans—although exceptions exist. Usually, they just run away.

Surprising a mother bear with cubs is one way to have a run-in with a black bear. If you encounter cubs, step back and give the family plenty of room to leave the area. Never get between a mother bear and her cubs.

The other opportunity for interspecies misunderstanding occurs on the subject of the rightful ownership of all that backpacking food you've been

Black bears are much smaller than grizzlies, but range in color from cinnamon to dark brown to almost black.

carrying. Bears in some popular national parks have lost their fear of humans, and can appear quite threatening.

Rangers in Yosemite National Park suggest that if a black bear seems overly interested in you or your food, you should wave your arms, make noise, get together with your hiking partner to appear more threatening, and even throw stones. (Not boulders! The point is to scare the animal away, not to injure it!)

Bear Language.

Q. If I see a grizzly bear in the backcountry, how do I know what to do? How can you tell if a bear is upset, angry, or getting ready to charge?

A. Most bear-human encounters proceed along the same lines: Human meets bear. Bear runs away.

Unless a grizzly bear is ill or a renegade (usually one that has been spoiled with too much contact with people and their food), it's usually not interested in causing trouble. Bears may, however, be defensive over their cubs or assertive about protecting a food source like carrion. In an encounter with a grizzly, try to back off to give it plenty of space. Do not look at it straight in the eye. Generally, if you give a bear plenty of space, it will retreat—but not always.

Bears, like humans, have a vast array of body language, and their body language actually looks a lot like ours. A bear that seems to be ignoring you is probably ignoring you. A bear that stands on its hind legs and sniffs the air is checking you out. An agitated bear that moves from side to side is getting way too upset for your safety. Pawing at the ground, drawing the lips back, and making a "popping" noise are indications that the bear will probably attack. Some attacks are bluff charges; some are for real. The bear may bluff several times. Do not run. You cannot outrun a bear, and running only incites its chase response. If possible, climb a tree. Adult grizzlies do not climb. Some hikers and backcountry rangers carry pepper spray in the backcountry to fend off bear attacks. It is considered to be an effective, if not infallible, defense. Wait until the bear is within range, then spray—and keep spraying—until it goes away. If you don't have spray, or it doesn't work, drop to the ground and play dead (see below).

The only exception to the "playing dead" rule is if the bear had been exhibiting predatory behavior, rather than defensive behavior. Predatory behavior is extremely rare. Examples would be if you were attacked while lying in your tent, or if the bear was actively stalking you before the attack. In those cases, experts recommend that you fight back with anything available, from your Swiss army knife to your ice ax.

Playing Dead.

Q. I've heard you're supposed to play dead if a grizzly bear attacks you. This seems unbelievable to me, not to mention impossible. Does it really work?

A. The prospect of lying in a terrified ball of fear while a bear takes a few swipes with a plate-sized claw (and let's not even think about those teeth) is unappealing, at best. But experts concur that it's the best way to survive a grizzly bear's charge.

The reason: The vast majority of grizzly bear attacks are defensive. The bear has for some reason become frightened or threatened. Its purpose in attacking you is to get rid of you as a threat. The theory is that if you play dead, the bear has achieved its goal and will go away. (After the attack, experts say to stay on the ground until you are sure the bear has left the area.)

The recommended position is to lie in a fetal position, with your knees drawn up to protect your vital organs, your head tucked, and your hands protecting the back of your neck. Hopefully, you're wearing your pack; it can protect your back.

Mountain Lions.

Q. I live in southern California, and there have been reports of mountain lion sightings nearby. Is it safe for my family and me to hike in lion country? What do I do if I see a mountain lion?

A. Count yourself lucky! Seeing a mountain lion is one of the great wildlife sightings in the American backcountry—and one of the most rare. Usually, the lion will see you long before you see it, and will slink off so quietly that the only evidence of its passing is a footprint.

No doubt mountain lions are intimidating: They weigh between 150 and 200 pounds, and average between 7 and 9 feet in overall length, although up to a third of that is tail. Mountain lions are tan, with black marks on the sides of the muzzle, the back of the ears, and the tip of the tail. They can jump as far as 20 feet. Despite their intimidating appearance, healthy lions in their natural habit don't prey on people. But lion habitat (and food supply) is shrinking. In recent years, there have been a few, thankfully still rare, attacks on people. Children and runners are most vulnerable—children, because they appear to be small, easy prey to a lion; runners, because it's in a cat's nature to chase things that run.

If you sense that a lion is looking at you with the expression of a hungry hiker staring at an all-you-can-eat pancake breakfast, give it plenty of space so it can reconsider and retreat, which is what it will usually do. If it exhibits threatening behavior or appears to be stalking you, try to make yourself look bigger. Flap your jacket and wave your arms. Get together with your hiking partner to make yourselves seem like a bigger adversary. If you are hiking with children, pick them up and keep them with you. Do not bend down (it makes you look smaller and more vulnerable). Do not turn your back on the lion.

Wildlife managers and rangers recommend that in the rare case of a lion attack, do *not* play dead or get into a fetal position (as you would with a grizzly bear). Instead, fight back—use your hiking stick, backpack, whatever you've got.

Saving the Wildlands.

Q. A few trips in the backcountry have taught me about both the beauty and the fragility of our wild places. I've especially noticed development creeping nearer the trails, and logging and other uses that impact the environment around the trails. What can I do?

A. Some of the natural phenomena discussed in this chapter are indeed under attack—from development, pollution, overuse, and irresponsible backcountry

An Appalachian Trail crew of volunteers: Preserving our trails means working for them.

behavior. Hikers often become advocates for the wildlands they love. Here are some easy ways to get started:

▲ Get in touch with trail groups that represent the trails you like to hike. Your membership supports their protection work, they will keep you apprised of new developments and threats and tell you how you can help. Local chapters of environmental organizations, and local groups that focus on regional issues also need a hand.

- Don't just sigh about the problem; do something. If your trail club asks members to write a letter to Congress, do it. Hikers have stopped roads from being built through recreation areas, and have influenced decisions on land use ranging from the building of ski resorts to windmill farms. Complain loudly and often—but direct your voice to the people who can do something.
- Teach others. Give presentations about trails and wildernesses in local schools. Share your experiences, your photos, and your love for the outdoors, and others will learn to share you passion.
- Practice Leave-No-Trace camping (see Chapter 8), and gently instruct others who may not know any better.

A Scottish "bothy" offers welcome shelter from damp weather on the Southern Upland Way.

Bibliography

Appalachian Trail Thru-Hikers' Companion. Appalachian Trail Conference (304-535-6331).

Berger, Karen. *Everyday Wisdom: 1001 Expert Tips for Hikers.* Seattle: The Mountaineers Books, 1997.

Berger, Karen, and Daniel R. Smith. *Where the Waters Divide: A 3,000-Mile Trek Along America's Continental Divide.* Woodstock, VT: Countryman Press, 1997.

Bruce, Dan. *The Thru-Hiker's Planning Guide.* Atlanta: Center for Appalachian Trail Studies, 2002.

Burns, Bob and Mike Burns. *Wilderness Navigation.* Seattle: The Mountaineers Books, 1999.

Demrow, Carl, and David Salisbury. *The Complete Guide to Trail Building and Maintenance.* City: Appalachian Mountain Club, 1998.

Graydon, Don, and Kurt Hanson. *Mountaineering: The Freedom of the Hills, 6th Edition.* Seattle: The Mountaineers Books, 1997.

Howe, Steve, Alan Kesselheim, Dennis Coello, and John Harlin III. *Making Camp: The Complete Guide for Hikers, Mountain Bikers, Paddlers & Skiers.* Seattle: The Mountaineers Books, 1997.

Hugo, Beverly. *Women and Thru-Hiking on the Appalachian Trail: Practical Advice from Hundreds of Women Long-Distance Hikers.* Insight Publishing Company, 2000.

Kjellstrom, Bjorn. *Be an Expert with Map and Compass: The Complete Orienteering Handbook.* Hoboken, NJ: John Wiley & Sons, 1994.

MacManiman, Gen. *Dry It, You'll Like It!* Fall City, WA: MacManiman, Inc., 2000.

McGiveney, Annette. *Leave No Trace: A Practical Guide to the New Wilderness Ethic.* Seattle: The Mountaineers Books, 1998.

Miller, Dorcas. *Backcountry Cooking: From Pack to Plate in 10 Minutes.* Seattle: The Mountaineers Books, 1997.

———. *More Backcountry Cooking: Moveable Feasts by the Experts.* Seattle: The Mountaineers Books, 2002.

Renner, Jeff. *Lightning Strikes: Staying Safe Under Stormy Skies.* Seattle: The Mountaineers Books, 2002.

Weiss, Eric. *Wilderness 911: A Step-by-Step Guide for Medical Emergencies and Improvised Care in the Backcountry.* Seattle: The Mountaineers Books, 1999.

The high altitudes of Colorado can be a strain for sea-level dwellers. Take time to acclimate.

Index

About the Author

Karen Berger writes full-time about travel, the outdoors, the environment, and especially backpacking. In the last 12 years she has walked more than 17,000 miles on six continents, and she is one of approximately twenty people who have thru-hiked the Appalachian Trail, the Pacific Crest Trail, and the Continental Divide Trail. She is a well-known and active member of the long-distance hiking community, and a successful magazine and book author. Her published books include *Along the Pacific Crest Trail* (Westcliffe), *Where the Waters Divide* (Harmony and Countryman), *Everyday Wisdom* (The Mountaineers Books), *Advanced Backpacking: A Trailside Guide* (Norton), *Hiking and Backpacking* (Norton), *SCUBA Diving: A Trailside Guide* (Norton), *The PCT: A Hiker's Companion* (Countryman), and *Hiking the Triple Crown: How to Hike America's Longest Trails* (The Mountaineers Books). Her magazine, newspaper, and Internet credits include *Backpacker, Scouting, GORP.com, Travelclassics.com, National Geographic Traveler, Islands, The New York Times*, and many others. You can visit her at *www.hikerwriter.com.*

The author and her husband, Dan Smith, in Grand Canyon National Park, Arizona.

THE MOUNTAINEERS, founded in 1906, is a nonprofit outdoor activity and conservation club, whose mission is "to explore, study, preserve, and enjoy the natural beauty of the outdoors. . . ." Based in Seattle, Washington, the club is now the third-largest such organization in the United States, with 15,000 members and five branches throughout Washington State.

The Mountaineers sponsors both classes and year-round outdoor activities in the Pacific Northwest, which include hiking, mountain climbing, ski-touring, snowshoeing, bicycling, camping, kayaking and canoeing, nature study, sailing, and adventure travel. The club's conservation division supports environmental causes through educational activities, sponsoring legislation, and presenting informational programs. All club activities are led by skilled, experienced volunteers, who are dedicated to promoting safe and responsible enjoyment and preservation of the outdoors.

If you would like to participate in these organized outdoor activities or the club's programs, consider a membership in The Mountaineers. For information and an application, write or call The Mountaineers, Club Headquarters, 300 Third Avenue West, Seattle, WA 98119; 206-284-6310.

The Mountaineers Books, an active, nonprofit publishing program of the club, produces guidebooks, instructional texts, historical works, natural history guides, and works on environmental conservation. All books produced by The Mountaineers Books fulfill the club's mission.

Send or call for our catalog of more than 500 outdoor titles:

The Mountaineers Books
1001 SW Klickitat Way, Suite 201
Seattle, WA 98134
800-553-4453
mbooks@mountaineersbooks.org
www.mountaineersbooks.org

The Mountaineers Books is proud to be a corporate sponsor of Leave No Trace, whose mission is to promote and inspire responsible outdoor recreation through education, research, and partnerships. The Leave No Trace program is focused specifically on human-powered (nonmotorized) recreation.

Leave No Trace strives to educate visitors about the nature of their recreational impacts, as well as offer techniques to prevent and minimize such impacts. Leave No Trace is best understood as an educational and ethical program, not as a set of rules and regulations.

For more information, visit *www.LNT.org*, or call 800-332-4100.

Other titles you might enjoy from The Mountaineers Books

Available at fine bookstores and outdoor stores, by phone at 800-553-4453, or at *www.mountaineersbooks.org*.

Everyday Wisdom: 1001 Expert Tips for Hikers by Karen Berger. $16.95 paperbound. 0-89886-523-9.

Backcountry Cooking: From Pack to Plate in 10 Minutes by Dorcas Miller. $16.95 paperbound. 0-89886-551-4.

More Backcountry Cooking: Moveable Feasts by the Experts by Dorcas Miller. $16.95 paperbound. 0-89886-900-5.

Day Hiker's Handbook: Get Started with the Experts by Mike Lanza. $16.95 paperbound. 0-89886-901-3.

Hiking the Triple Crown by Karen Berger. $18.95 paperbound. 0-89886-760-6.

Wilderness 911: A Step-by-Step Guide for Medical Emergencies and Improvised Care in the Backcountry by Eric A. Weiss, M.D. $16.95 paperbound. 0-89886-597-2.

Making Camp: A Complete Guide for Hikers, Mountain Bikers, Paddlers & Skiers by Steve Howe, Alan Kesselheim, Dennis Coello, and John Harlin. $16.95 paperbound. 0-89886-522-0.

Leave No Trace: A Guide to the New Wilderness Etiquette by Annette McGivney. $16.95 paperbound. 0-89886-522-0.

Don't Get Sick: The Hidden Dangers of Camping and Hiking by Buck Tilton, M.S., and Rick Bennett, Ph.D. $8.95 paperbound. 0-89886-854-8.

Secrets of Warmth: For Comfort or Survival by Hal Weiss. $11.95 paperbound. 0-89886-643-X.

Staying Found: The Complete Map & Compass Handbook, 3rd Edition by June Fleming. $12.95 paperbound. 0-89886- 785-1.

Wilderness Navigation: Finding Your Way Using Map, Compass, Altimeter, & GPS by Mike Burns and Bob Burns. $9.95 paperbound. 0-89886-629-4.

GPS Made Easy: Using Global Positioning Systems in the Outdoors, 3rd Edition by Lawrence Letham. $14.95 paperbound. 0-89886-802-5.

Backcountry Bear Basics: The Definitive Guide to Avoiding Unpleasant Encounters by David Smith. $10.95 paperbound. 0-89886-500-X.

Outdoor Leadership: Technique, Common Sense & Self-Confidence by John Graham. $16.95 paperbound. 0-89886-502-6.

Conditioning for Outdoor Fitness: A Comprehensive Training Guide by David Musnick, M.D. and Mark Pierce, A.T.C. $21.95 paperbound. 0-89886-450-X.

Photography Outdoors: A Field Guide for Travel & Adventure Photographers, 2nd Edition by Mark Gardner and Art Wolfe. $14.95 paperbound. 0-89886-888-2.